South Australia
horizons beyond

· Colour essay by Tony Baker · Black and white interviews by Megan Lloyd ·
· Short fiction by David Gibb · Design by Liz Nicholson ·
· Photography by leading South Australian photographers ·

two degrees of separation

As a child, growing up in the South Australian bush, I was always aware of that distant presence: The City. There was only one City, a far-off magical place always spoken of in hushed tones, and always apparently spelt with a capital, along with other fabled lands such as Disneyland or Oz.

School holidays, above all else, meant a trip to The City, and an extended stay with grandparents of limitless generosity and tolerance. The City meant Television, of course – but there were other joys that remain in my mind in a sort of mental upper-case, as befits magical things. There was The Zoo and The Glenelg Tram. There was The Royal Show, and its attendant joys: Show-Bags, Ghost-Trains, Ferris-Wheels. There was The Museum, especially its crypt-like Egyptian Room, stuffed with mummies, sarcophagi, mysteriously inscribed tablets, and other graveyard loot.

Holidays also meant The Pictures (not yet become the movies) and long afternoons of Batman, Tarzan, Fantales and Jaffas. In the bush we were still restricted to the wireless (not yet become radio). In some cinemas the pictures played around the clock – I felt I could walk out of *Around the World in Eighty Days* at the end of one long Christmas holiday, and return to pick up the thread, mid-Pacific or on a collapsing suspension bridge, a year later.

The Airport was another important attraction. It was a sacred site to my grandfather, Australia's first bikie and a worshipper of all things mechanical. The high point of our visits was to climb to the balcony and watch the propeller blades splutter to life, one after the other, on the old Electras and DC6s and Viscounts. Grandpa was also a great fan of the Melbourne Express, which he would take me to watch each night as it thundered through one or another local level crossing.

'Feel the suction!' he would shout, as we stood perilously close to the tracks. At his most inspired, he would race the express to the next crossing, passing just in front of the onrushing locomotive as the signals clanged terrifyingly.

Those childhood pleasures have lost some of their magic for me now, but The City still seems full of singularity: a place still described reverently, in upper-case, with free use of the definite article.

The Museum still deserves a visit, both the old Egyptian Room, and the collection of Aboriginal artifacts which is the best there is. The Information Office is a great help to those who like to collect things. It's worth looking under rocks in Adelaide, and taking whatever might be lurking there to the Museum for identification.

The Hills are indispensible. Interminable compulsory Sunday drives into the Hills were part of every South Australian's upbringing in the fifties and sixties, but the valley-towns and hilltop pubs and restaurants and waterfalls and gorges all seem much closer now.

The Beach! Adelaide's ten-mile long beach is unlike others. There is never any surf, unless a Hobie Cat passes too close. The sand is terrific, however. It might not be a macho beach, suitable for kicking into faces, but I've constructed some mighty fine sandcastles there. For those not interested in high-rise sand, skinny-dipping and skinny-baking are possible further south at Maslins Beach, and surfing that is adequately life-threatening can be tackled another half an hour beyond that, at Waitpinga or Boomer.

So much for the institutions. What of the people? Some locals still smart over the eastern states' caricature of the Athens of the South as a city of opera-loving wine soaks – if only because of the kernels of truth. There are about 365 restaurants and cafes; an ideal figure for those intending to stay a year. From Montefiore Hill the former city of churches is revealed now as a city of restaurants, boutiques and night-clubs, the steeples and spires of which can be seen everywhere, summoning the faithful.

How have I avoided mentioning The Wineries so far? Wineries are inescapable, having the city of Adelaide surrounded on three sides. On the fourth side lies the ocean. The city can't be left by any route – except raft or airlift – without having to pass countless cellar-doors. Fond hope of fleeing without a case stuffed in the boot!

Still on the subject of upper-case pleasures, I should genuflect in the direction of Culture, whose mainstream versions revolve around The Festival and the Festival Centre. But also – The Fringe! And, from 1998, the *Ring Cycle*. The City is home to the excellent Elder Conservatorium, and performance music of great variety. In the East End on a Sunday afternoon, writers, artists and actors can always be spotted sitting spilling coffee and gelati over the dailies as they search for reviews of themselves, their friends, their enemies.

A curious thing about Adelaide is that any one of its million inhabitants will know someone who knows you. Two degrees of separation is usual – everyone connects, somehow.

I prefer to spend Sunday afternoons on a Tennis-court. John Cheever once wrote a famous story in which a citizen of an upper middle-class Long Island suburb decides to swim home from a party, cross-country, through a succession of neighbouring swimming-pools. It's probably possible to run a tennis-court line-marker from the ocean in Adelaide to the Hills, jumping from court to court. And on arriving in the Hills, to pick up a racquet and play one last game.

Nestled in a corner of many South Australian minds, along with precious memories of The Egyptian Room (and semi-precious memories of compulsory Sunday Afternoon Drives), are memories of picnics or tennis in Belair National Park, in some far-off Golden Summer, the thick dusty sunlight, Hans Heysen light, filtering through the big spotted eucalypts.

Dostoevsky wrote that the best education is a single precious memory from childhood: among mine are those sun-denched late summer afternoons of tennis and food and conversation, an essence of Adelaide.

Peter Goldsworthy

contents

part 1 changing worlds

1 A place in the sun 10 • 'As a mob we are rich in our culture' 18 • 'Go down any Adelaide street and you see multiculturalism at work' 24 • **2** A light shines in a constellation 30 • 'A place that is vibrant and where you want to be' 42 • Just visiting 48 • **3** A mosaic of a state 50 • 'Adelaide could be the wildlife capital of Australia' 62 • **4** The shark and the ark 68 • Frogman 78 • 'The everyday person actually cares about the environment' 80 •

part 2 creative energy

5 Cuisine of the southern sun 88 • 'A lot of people are coming to South Australia for food experiences' 96 • **6** The wines of the century 104 • 'With wine, we haven't even begun to do what we can do' 116 • The cyclist 122 • **7** A festive kind of place 124 • 'In the arts, it's about being prepared to invent and follow ideas fearlessly' 140 • E-mail from Harry 146 • 'The film crews are returning to the streets' 148 • **8** Sport in the south 154 • 'Whoever said sport was more than a religion must have visited South Australia' 162 •

part 3 quiet dynamism

'South Australia attracts more research funding, per capita, than any other state' 170 • Su Song's journey 176 • 'When IT companies learn to export, boy are they going to be dangerous!' 178 • **9** On the cusp 184 • 'The future of manufacturing is based on new ideas, new methods, new products' 192 • **10** Wide horizons 200 • 'South Australian farmers have a proud history of thinking outside the square' 210 • Mailman and the miner 216 • 'Mining is not for the faint-hearted but there are great prizes out there' 218 •

Postscripts – Megan Lloyd 226 • Tony Baker 227 •

changing worlds

a place in

You can walk central Adelaide in a single morning. Within that compass you will pass olive groves, parklands with flocks of parrots and one of the prettiest racecourses in Australia.

A Parliament House and a Government House, each imposing but far from grandiose, face each other across the main boulevard. Less than a minute from the parliament is a casino housed within a railway station so grand its construction nearly bankrupted the state. A few minutes' stroll from the Government House, past a network of galleries and museums and a mall of department stores, boutiques and arcades, is a street lined with restaurants, pubs and cafes, many of them on the site of a former produce market with an ornate facade appropriately depicting a cornucopia.

Everything is looking up for this young man at Streaky Bay | GRANT NOWELL

There are two universities, a third in the suburbs beyond, and unspoilt nineteenth-century villas and mansions adorned with the intricate ironwork known as Adelaide lace.

On two sides of the main square, said to be the size of the Place de la Concorde in Paris, are the administrative centre of the state government and the court buildings. A moment's walk takes you to another street of restaurants and as colourful, aromatic and polyglot a market as you will find anywhere. This ability to move between worlds is the essence of Adelaide.

A tram ride from that same square will take you to Glenelg and one of the magnificent white-sand beaches that are Adelaide's western garland. Head east instead and you are soon in folded hills studded with eucalypts, apple and pear orchards, market gardens and vineyards.

Leave this metropolis of a million people and you are in what elsewhere on the planet might be entirely different countries and climates.

From South Australia come half of the nation's wines, the best half. Some of the vines are planted in the south-east near giant pine forests and a world heritage cave complex filled with the fossils of extinct giant kangaroos and marsupial lions. Others line the banks of Australia's largest river – once again a highway for paddleboats – where groves of citrus, apricots and peaches ripen in the sun.

Off the beaches of Victor Harbor, and in the waters of

Above: On the road at Arkaroola in the Flinders Ranges ADAM BRUZZONE

the Great Australian Bight, pods of whales nurture their young before making the long journey back to Antarctica.

Australia as it was before the arrival of Europeans and their plants and animals is best seen on Kangaroo Island, only a hop away from Adelaide, where sea lions laze on the beaches and penguins nest in the rocky outcrops.

To the north, beyond the sprawling wheatlands and the grandeur of the Flinders Ranges, is the desert outback. Here is the Australia of lonely homesteads on cattle and sheep stations the size of a city. But this ocean of red sand also yields copper, gold, uranium, natural gas and – from what looks like the terrestrial version of a moonscape – opals, the blazing jewels that are fire from the desert.

To travel South Australia, as elsewhere on the continent, is to realise why its landscapes have so gripped the imagination of painters that each generation strives to define and celebrate them anew.

Adelaide's climate is usually described, with reasonable accuracy, as Mediterranean. I like the word for another reason. As the Roman Empire declined and legions were withdrawn to defend the capital, around the shores of the Mediterranean developed cities and colonies that, for all that they had in common, displayed strong local identities and cultures. Evolving in their own right, and responding to new forces remaking the world, they became much more than outposts of an empire.

The British Empire was much bigger than the Roman; its twilight and collapse were far swifter. You might think it a fanciful parallel, but here, long after the abandonment of the British Empire, is a state on its furthest boundary that owes much to the founding imperialists yet is profoundly different from them. It is changing and being remade at a pace that no empire-builder at the start of the millennium could have comprehended.

This may help explain why South Australia approaches the new century with such a curious and characteristic mixture of confidence, complacency and trepidation. There would be less anxiety if more of its people knew its quietly stirring history and so appreciated that another characteristic mixture – luck and enterprise – has prevailed over much greater strains and challenges.

Each society likes to think of itself as somehow different and South Australians are no exception. Unlike most other Australian states, the colony did not begin as a penal dumping ground. Adelaide was shaped by the theories of the first of a line of adventurers, Edward Gibbon Wakefield. Instead of granting land to settlers, Wakefield proposed that a government-backed company would sell sections of land and the money would fund the migration of free settlers.

On 28 December 1836 a shipload of officials and colonists who had voyaged halfway across the world gathered on the Glenelg sands to proclaim the new colony. In doing so they dispossessed the Aboriginal Australians whose ancestors had occupied the continent for at least 40,000 years. In the Adelaide region they were the Kaurna, pronounced Garna, people. Other groups lived as hunter-gatherers across South Australia right into the heart of the most forbidding northern deserts.

The newcomers were mainly English, with a leavening of German dissenters who would have a disproportionate economic and cultural influence. These pioneers were resourceful, ambitious and quarrelsome. A mid-twentieth century historian, Douglas Pike, summed it up in the title of his study of the period: *Paradise of Dissent*.

The settlers were imaginative and had a capacity for the grand design. They came to make money and fortunes would be made, although in the early years it seemed that ruin would be a more likely fate. They also brought as part of their mental luggage a reformist nonconformism, in a general as well as strictly religious sense, that would provide another persistent strand in the South Australian story.

While this book is the portrait of a place on the cusp of a millennium and not a formal history, to look around the city and state today is to see an abundance of evidence of what was decided in the first decades. It is tangible in the case of the landscapes and striking in the fabric and architecture of Adelaide.

They were tempestuous times. In the 1840s South Australia teetered on a financial precipice until it was saved,

Harvesting olives at McLaren Vale

and then transformed, by the discovery of vast copper deposits. Then, in the 1850s, the colony was nearly depopulated by the lure of the Victorian gold-rush, before its people turned gold fever to their own advantage as suppliers of provisions to the diggers and buyers of their bullion.

In a similar way, the devastation of the Victorian vineyards in the late nineteenth century spurred the growth of South Australian winemaking, an industry that still contributes to the state's distinctive character.

In the 1990s the South Australian State Bank had to be rescued with a mountain of taxpayers' money; more than three billion dollars of it. Yet within five years the talk was again of growth and better times ahead. Few people seemed to appreciate how much this resembled one of those symphonies in which the themes recur, slightly different each time but immediately recognisable.

One other aspect of today's South Australia goes generally unremarked because it is so much taken for granted. It is such a safe place in the sun. The statement should be qualified. There is crime, and some crimes have been atrocious and bizarre. But there is normally no need for anyone to be more than mildly prudent. There are bigots and, although a South Australian government led the way in returning vast tracts of land to Aboriginal ownership, too many Aboriginal people live difficult lives. These caveats made, you return to that sense of security.

Here is a place of just under a million square kilometres

with a congenial climate of four distinct seasons, average summer temperature on the coast around 28 degrees and in winter 15 degrees, dry but with sufficient rainfall. Pollution is minimal and the environment protected.

South Australia is multicultural and multiracial without serious communal tensions. Descendants of migrants from the United Kingdom make up the largest ethnic group in the state, but the traditions, music, dress and food of nearly 100 other ethnic groups – from Afghan to Zimbabwean – co-exist in the cultural landscape. One in four South Australians was born overseas. The state has attracted more refugees than any other in Australia. South Australia pioneered education in community languages. The state has had an Aboriginal Governor – Australia's first and only; Adelaide has had a Greek Lord Mayor and many Italian and other European and Asian local councillors.

The only complaint about South Australia's style of parliamentary democracy is from electors who think they are required to vote too often for too many representatives. The right of property is fiercely upheld and guaranteed by an independent judiciary. There is little corruption, and the only curbs on free speech are those laid down by law. As with the rest of Australia there is no conceivable external threat.

Within South Australia's borders you can be part of a bustling state capital or you can be alone from horizon to horizon.

Shopping in Adelaide Arcade

'As a mob we are rich in our culture'

In 1966, when Australia switched from the English pound to decimal currency, South Australia passed what was viewed then as ground-breaking legislation recognising Aboriginal rights. In the same year, Katrina Power's mother stood up in an Adelaide court room to prove a white man was the father of her daughter.

For an Aboriginal woman – then without even the right to vote – it took great courage to prove paternity. Maintenance was awarded by the court but never paid. Thirty-one years later, Power has never met her father.

Welcoming dance by the Paitya company for a new dance ground at Tauondi College in Port Adelaide | NICI CUMPSTON

'I draw great strength from the fact that my mum had the courage – when society didn't even count her, when black women were being ripped off the streets and accused of soliciting – to say: "This is what he did and I'm going to make him accountable,"' Power says.

'I've grown up totally in a black environment and I don't give my white father any credit. We say Aboriginality is about spirituality not the colour of your skin.'

Power, 32, is a descendant of the original inhabitants of the Adelaide plain, the Kaurna people, and the Narungga people from Yorke Peninsula. She was brought up by her maternal grandparents in Adelaide's north-west suburbs, in a family of twelve 'in a traditionally overcrowded house – porridge for breakfast, Ma and Pa Kettle stuff. I loved it.'

Unlike many of her contemporaries, Power finished secondary school, taking a part-time job at 15 to support herself in quieter, study-friendly surroundings, and enrolled in a teaching diploma. This was interrupted by the death of her beloved grandfather, Charles Agius: 'I guess I went walkabout for a while after that and needed time out. As I was approaching adulthood, I lost the single most important figure in my life.

'He was such a great man and I find now, even though fourteen years have passed, I feel his influence on me, *very strongly*. He helped co-found the Aboriginal Lands Trust, which was the first lands trust in Australia, and the irony of that is the Lands Trust owns Tandanya.'

Power, a former journalist turned Aboriginal arts worker, was the youngest person appointed to the board of the Tandanya Aboriginal Cultural Institute – the nation's sole Aboriginal cultural centre, based in Adelaide – and at just 29 was made its chair, a position she still holds. 'I feel there's this great sense of continuity between my grandfather's presence and my own. There were a lot of older fellas on the board who were his confidantes. Here was another connection. I remember him yarning with these people, talking politics twenty years before. So, they became a part of my life too. It was enlightening and enriching.'

Power's 'walkabout' after her grandfather's death led to an association with the Aboriginal Affairs departments of both the state and federal governments and first-hand contact with Aborigines living traditionally in South Australia's desert and west coast. It was an 'eye-opener' for a young Aboriginal, or nunga, girl brought up in the city.

'We are born with an instant respect for those people and an envy too – for a life that might have been, a life that could be. It was just magic. So simple, you know: survival rather than acquisition of possessions. I had an incredible sense of belonging and I was welcomed into the country.'

In Australia's bicentennial year, 1988, Power applied for and was given a newspaper cadetship – the first nunga to be hired by Adelaide's only daily newspaper, the *Advertiser*. 'I rocked up to the editor and said: "Look, I reckon I can do this. Can you give me a go?"' After more

overseas, she decided to concentrate on her baby daughter and turned to freelancing as an agent for Aboriginal musicians and dancers.

Power and another Aboriginal arts worker, Sonja Arnold, set up the Australian Indigenous Performing Arts Coalition, which became known as Narna Tarkendi (Kaurna for 'The Door Is Open'). 'No festival seems complete without some indigenous participation. We capitalised on that,' Power says. The pair lined up artists for events such as the biennial international music festival Womadelaide, and took dance and music groups on overseas tours.

Power has continued to appear regularly in print through her former paper's Letters to the Editor page, where she consistently puts an Aboriginal perspective. She once kissed the Duchess of Kent on a tour of Tandanya, and lectured her on the need for Australia to become a republic.

'Australia has got to cut the umbilical cord. A wise old black woman said this to me: "If I forget the past, I lose one eye. If I dwell on the past, I lose two eyes."'

Both in speech and writing, Power's own voice is eloquent, incisive, passionate and persuasive. 'To be born black in Australia is to be born with a political handicap,' she once said. 'But while as individuals we may be the poorest of the poor, as a mob we are rich in our culture and priceless in protecting our environment.'

It is this rich and sophisticated culture, largely unknown to younger Aborigines, that Power believes holds the future for her people. 'More than 70 per cent of international tourists who come to Australia cite an interest in Aboriginal culture as one of their reasons for coming here,' she says. 'Many more people overseas appreciate that Australian Aboriginals are the oldest living civilisation than Australians do. We know the Aboriginal industry is worth hundreds of millions of dollars to the Australian economy.

'Particularly in South Australia, where you've got the desert, the river, anything you want in the country can be found and there are stories to tell. Better to have a black fella telling you the story than reading it out of a white book.

'The key to growth for anyone is self-esteem and being proud of who you are, believing in yourself, your gifts and

Kevin O'Loughlin explains the Tjilbruke story at Aldinga

that you have something positive to contribute. So, we are saying this is an opportunity to maximise on our own individual spirit, while creating employment and economic opportunities that would not normally be available to us. The crucial component of cultural development is the rejuvenation of the spirit. The economic spinoffs from that are just a bonus.'

Power acknowledges that history records South Australia as a leader in positive initiatives for its indigenous population – establishing the first Aboriginal Women's Council, the first Aboriginal Lands Trust, the first Aboriginal school (in 1986). 'We've been significant movers. While we seem to be drowned by our eastern states counterparts, South Australia has a proud record.' Paternalistic and restrictive legislation was repealed in the 1960s and landmark land laws were passed in the 1980s with wide public support. More than 10,000 square kilometres of land in the state's north-west was entrusted to the Pitjantjatjara people, and another 10,000 in the Great Victoria Desert in an area known as Maralinga.

In recent times, though, South Australia and the rest of the country have become embroiled in a string of emotion-charged issues as black and white Australia grapple with co-existence. Continually scratching at the nation's scab have been debates about Aboriginal rights and access to

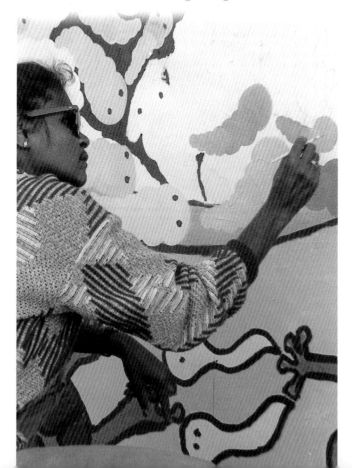

Shireen Hightold working on a mural at Rosewater

Black Australians need white Australians to acknowledge their pain. How can we heal unless you say, "You have endured pain." We need to see Aboriginal studies made compulsory in all schools. We will never have reconciliation until we have an appreciation for each other's cultures, values and differences.'

Power has recently moved her young family three hours north of Adelaide to Port Augusta, which has Australia's second-largest Aboriginal community, and where English is often the second language spoken. 'I'm interested in travelling into the desert and getting back into Aboriginal communities if I can,' she says. 'I'm taking it slowly. I'm really a foreigner here. I want to be a nobody and just learn.'

land, protecting sacred sites, deaths in custody and the 'stolen' children, generations forcibly taken from their Aboriginal mothers right up until 1972.

'We taught Aboriginal mothers only one generation ago that they were not capable of bringing up their children. Now, we are seeing the victims of these laws.

'How can you point the finger at young black kids and say, "You've got to stay at school," if these children's parents were not educated and they do not understand that it's their responsibility to care for their children because the law previously said, "You can't."

'People are saying, "Why should I be guilty for that?"'

'Go down any Adelaide street and you see multiculturalism at work.'

'People today can have their own cultural identity and still see themselves as part of a wider Australia. There is no contradiction at all,' says Viv Szekeres, director of South Australia's Migration Museum in Adelaide.

The fact that the state has Australia's first museum devoted to the history and traditions of its immigrants says much about its support for multiculturalism. Szekeres herself is an immigrant, arriving in the 1970s from England, although she has an Eastern European background.

Buddhist Community Temple at Ottoway | ERIC ALGRA

Szekeres and Migration Museum curator Kate Walsh believe that because South Australia was designed as a free colony with no convicts, its immigrants came with a different outlook, which later shaped Adelaide's reputation as both a conservative city and a town of liberal social thinkers. 'Our tradition of free-thinking comes from the way the colony was founded,' says Walsh. 'Because churches were not seen to dominate the establishment, the voices of ordinary people could be heard.'

Szekeres says, 'Most of the people willing to leave Britain or Europe were coming from industries that were struggling, like the miners in Cornwall, or they were coming from major cities experiencing great problems.' The first immigrant settlers to arrive in South Australia were English, Scottish, Welsh, Cornish, Irish and German, with a smattering of other nationalities. 'The first Italian was here in about 1841,' Walsh says, 'but you don't really get large numbers until the 1890s and 1900s.'

'A few Scandinavians jumped ship,' Szekeres adds, 'Lebanese traders, a few Chinese, handfuls of Polish . . . because East Prussia, where the Germans were coming from, is very near the Polish border.'

These first groups had a strong impact on the colony's culture. The Cornish and Welsh created a mining industry; the English and Germans went into farming and

Ceremony performed by Steve Goldsmith

Buddhist Community Temple | ERIC ALGRA

Adelaide Mosque | ERIC ALGRA

By 1901, when Australia became a federation, South Australia's official population was roughly 90 per cent British and 10 per cent German, the latter living in their own close-knit communities. The federal parliament lost no time passing the Immigration Restriction Act, dubbed the 'White Australia Policy', which remained in force until the 1960s. There were various immigration schemes to subsidise migration from Britain. The idea was 'populate or perish' as the country trembled at its isolation from the rest of the English-speaking world.

'South Australia was part of the British Empire and saw itself as such,' says Szekeres. 'Nobody questioned that English should be the main language or that English

horticulture, heading into the Barossa region, for example, and starting the state's wine industry. They built houses and organised the land the way it was at home. They unpacked their traditional skills and approaches to life.

This had a profound impact on the local Aboriginal population, Szekeres says. 'The impact was without a doubt negative. You just can't pretend it wasn't.' Walsh adds, 'It was the influence of Christianity, the loss of access to the land, the devastation of numbers through introduced illness.'

Szekeres: 'And also, I'm afraid, the poisoning of wells and flour and God knows what else ... and the deliberate going out and getting rid of people, shooting. You can't hide it.'

customs, law, traditions, regalia, sport or manners should dominate. When South Australia went into the First World War, people agreed that they would be there to fight for the "home" country, even though that meant terrible things for the local German population.'

'Up until the Depression and the Second World War, you do have Greeks, Italians and Bulgarians coming to South Australia, particularly in the late 1920s,' says Walsh, but there were no subsidies for non-British immigrants until the 1950s. 'They often worked for market gardeners, for instance, and then saved up and bought their own land. The Bulgarians were very active in draining the swampy land around Fulham Gardens [in Adelaide's west] and developing their own market gardens.

'Some of the Italians in the 1920s were involved in the terrazzo and concrete industries, some were working on market gardens and buying their own land. Some had cafes and urban-based jobs. Greeks were often city-oriented. It's not huge numbers, but enough to create communities.'

The most intense period of migration to South Australia came in the aftermath of the Second World War. Australia accepted about 180,000 displaced Europeans.

Most of these immigrant adults went into manual labour in factories, roadworks, railways, forests and hospitals – yet many were well-educated professionals. 'Most were never able to resume their professions,' Szekeres says. 'They had to learn English and retrain from the beginning. Most gave up and decided to see their children through instead.'

Walsh: 'They arrived with virtually nothing, a suitcase. For them it was about getting a house, furniture, a car, the essentials of life in suburban Australia.'

The new arrivals did not give up their cultural identity, however. They immediately formed clubs and associations. 'Choral, dance, theatre groups – one of their first moves was to re-establish these, in order to overcome the loneliness and sense of displacement many of them experienced,' Walsh says.

Industries were built on the back of migrant labour. But Australia wanted more immigrants, especially British ones. The federal government's £10 assisted-passage scheme was set up to to attract Britons, particularly those with big families. 'They even said they wanted ten British migrants for every "foreigner",' Szekeres says. 'The only problem was that Britain was recovering from war by the late 1950s and 1960s and was becoming a much nicer place to live. So the Australian government started to make agreements with other countries – Germany, Holland, Malta, Italy and Greece.'

Walsh: 'Particularly Germany and the Netherlands, for South Australia. A lot of Dutch people came to Adelaide and lived in the Elizabeth area.' Elizabeth, now a suburb in Adelaide's north, was a city created for migrants – mainly British – providing not only their housing but also their jobs at big industrial plants like the Holden automobile works.

The migrants of the 1950s and 1960s had an immediate impact on South Australia. 'If you talk to any of them they'll say that they felt they were being pushed to forget their past and to become "Australians",' Szekeres says. 'But if you look at needs as basic as diet, they couldn't bear it. They started importing coffee beans, particular pastas, and bit by bit they started setting up industries here to make pastas, grow capsicums and so on. Australians will tell you they'd never seen capsicums, broccoli or zucchinis in the 1950s. Gradually the nature of the Australian diet began to change. These migrants had a huge impact on the way we eat and just about every aspect of life.' Walsh agrees: 'Education, the arts, manufacturing industries, whether they were using their own skills or working as unskilled labourers, they played a role in the development of South Australia.'

A string of events in the 1970s – the abandonment of the White Australia Policy, the Vietnam and Cambodian wars, conflicts in Latin America, South America and Sri Lanka – led to migrants coming from all over the world. Until recently British migrants were by far the largest single group; New Zealanders are now the single biggest national group moving to South Australia.

With its tiny Chinese-born population, Adelaide was the last mainland Australian capital to have a 'Chinatown'. There are only about 10,000 Vietnamese-born people in South Australia, yet already they have started to make their presence felt, opening shops and restaurants and particularly market gardens. Vietnamese South Australians grow 80 per cent of the state's cucumbers.

'People bring in their traditions and culture, which are then also gradually changed by the Australian environment,' says Szekeres. 'All those activities filter into our society and enrich life in various ways. We are totally optimistic about South Australia's future. We see the evidence daily – people getting on with their lives. Go down any Adelaide street and you see multiculturalism at work.'

a light shines

When the English actor Wilfred Hyde White was performing in Adelaide, each evening he would be driven from his Hindley Street hotel to Her Majesty's Theatre. As the car passed Light Square, where the city's founder-planner is buried and memorialised by a marble column topped with a surveyor's theodolite, Hyde White would doff his hat and say: 'Good on you, Colonel. You did a fine job.' It was a fitting tribute, for while Adelaide is named after the queen who was William IV's consort, it is really Light's city.

William Light was the greatest of the European adventurers who have beached on South Australian shores. By the time he arrived as the first surveyor-general he had already had a colourful career. He was born in Penang, in what is now Malaysia, the son of the city's founder, Francis, and his mistress Marthina, who was probably Malay Portuguese. William served with gallantry in the Peninsula War, fought in the Spanish revolutionary war and commanded a ship in Mohammed Ali's Egyptian navy. He was a great man: soldier, seaman, artist and musician as well as surveyor.

Colonel Light's statue points to the city from Montefiore Hill in North Adelaide | SA TOURISM/ADAM BRUZZONE

On 7 February 1837 Light completed his finest work, a sketch plan for the town of Adelaide. His roving life had exposed him to many cities, and he seems to have drawn on a variety of sources. The crowning flourish of his original genius was the 930 hectares of parkland that border Adelaide as its pastoral frame.

The city was divided into two, north and south, separated by the shallow valley of the Torrens River. North Adelaide was segmented into 342 one-acre blocks. The city square mile comprised 700 single-acre blocks on a grid pattern aerated by wide streets. The plan was given harmony by five garden squares: Victoria, the central one, embellished by statues and a fountain, and four satellites, Whitmore, Hindmarsh, Hurtle and Light. North Adelaide was given Wellington Square.

Light anticipated modern town-planning principles. Not until Walter Burley Griffin created the national capital, Canberra, would anything so bold and daring be seen in Australia again. Those familiar with both cities give the palm to Light.

Virtually from its conception Adelaide has been a city-state. Almost three out of four South Australians live in metropolitan Adelaide and its suburbs. The city is a political, judicial, commercial and cultural centre as well as a place for shopping, living and, more recently, tourism. As the new century nears there are anxieties that Adelaide will join other cities suffering the doughnut effect of a hollowing centre amid thriving outer suburbs with enormous shopping malls. Perhaps; but I suspect this is a case of distinctly premature obituary writing that fails to take account of Adelaide's multiple personalities. The city is more than a nine-to-five CBD. It is South Australia's heart, a beating heart thanks to Colonel Light who, in the words of historian Archibald Grenfell Price, 'carried out the most successful and permanent work in the story of the colony'.

Part of Adelaide's appeal is the ease with which you can move between its worlds. This can be vividly depicted in the career of one of the city's eminent modern sons, John Jefferson Bray. Dr Bray, who died in 1995, was a barrister who became chief justice, a classical scholar, a chancellor of the University of Adelaide, and a poet who read his work aloud at Adelaide arts festivals. He was also a gregarious man who relished the pub life. He lived in the city, first in Hutt Street, later in Hurtle Square. A day in the life of John Bray might have seen him walk to his Supreme Court chambers, visit the State Library and head on to the nearby university before downing a few beers at a city hotel and walking home. He had at least four careers and an international reputation yet, save for taking a tram to go swimming at Glenelg, he hardly ever crossed the parklands. Dr Bray's life was not typical, but it was illustrative.

Another pleasing facet of Adelaide is its architectural mix, partly the result of luck, partly of design. A skyline of tall buildings, the more extravagant the better, has become the modern equivalent of ancient city walls. A city is just not properly urban otherwise. Adelaide has a skyline, its individual elements making it easily recognisable. Especially when illuminated by the golden light of one of

foreground the twin fifty-metre spires of St Peter's Anglican Cathedral look over Adelaide Oval, one of the prettiest sports grounds on earth, next to what is now the Torrens Lake. The river, which dwindled to a series of waterholes in

its spring or autumn evenings, it has a particular grandeur. What can still catch my breath after almost thirty years of watching it grow is that this is grandeur on a human scale.

From a vantage point in North Adelaide, looking south, we can see the way we are and how it happened. In the

summer, has been dammed since 1881. It glides under bridges, past boathouses and through parks and gardens.

Looking from west to east, right to left, are the convention and exhibition centres next to the squat pile of the Hyatt Regency Hotel. Together they make one of those

Adelaide cityscape

giant construction projects of the unstoppable – or so it seemed – 1980s. In front of the railway station-cum-casino and the solid grey of Parliament House is that 1970s monument to Adelaide's ambitions and aspirations, the massive tower of the former State Bank and the shopping complex at the western end of Rundle Mall. These are what remain of the latest boom to have proved as unsinkable as the *Titanic*.

gleaming white, angular Festival Centre. With Government House across the road, here is the nucleus of Adelaide.

Over-reaching the hodgepodge of hotel, bank and insurance towers and the more assertive survivors of the first great public building boom of the 1870s are the

I like to think of North Terrace from King William Street west to the Botanic Gardens as the dividend of a trunkload of books. The 117 books came with the 1836 settlers. They, together with high-minded citizens, seeded the first institutes, which found a permanent home in 1860 on the corner of North Terrace and Kintore Avenue. From this grew a government policy of providing space in these original northern parklands for cultural and educational bodies, so today this stretch of North Terrace is Adelaide's cultural boulevard. Museums, art gallery, library and university are mostly housed in their handsomely restored or maintained original buildings, and most of them are still sufficiently mindful of their origins and obligations not to charge for admission.

The Botanic Gardens provide a green cornerstone to all this civic enterprise – and the ornate hotel opposite provides a fine counterpoint. Even in the gardens high-mindedness is all around you. There are flowers but the emphasis is on the botanical, not the playful, so the effect is of a hundred shades of green. Here too is another engaging contrast with which to end this city scan. The steel-and-glass palm house conservatory in the gardens shows how the Victorian era could be elegant as well as solemn. As part of Australia's bicentennial celebrations it was complemented by a tropical conservatory on the gardens' eastern perimeter. Inside the geometric arc of the building, maintained with a technology that is an achievement in itself, is a small but complete rainforest. The driest state in the driest inhabited continent, runs a familiar Adelaide tag. So what do we give ourselves as a birthday present? A rainforest. To understand that and its implications is to begin to understand what makes Adelaide tick.

After fondly extolling Adelaide as the hub it is no paradox to add that it is also a constellation of villages. After all, the place began in one – since Glenelg is as much dormitory village as resort.

Colonel Light envisaged a canal linking Port Adelaide and the city and he provided the skeleton for what became the surrounding leafy suburbs. The growth was evolutionary. Shipping gave early Port Adelaide almost as many stately commercial buildings – and pubs – as the city ten kilometres away.

Shipping has changed but the maritime atmosphere lives on and it is still a quiet pleasure to amble around the Port. Optimists have been proclaiming a Port renaissance for a generation, but economic reality has been a terrific conservator.

Today, though, it seems the revival is actually happening, quietly and tastefully; more people, more restaurants and other amenities. Together with another renewal along the beach suburbs between Port Adelaide and Glenelg, this is giving the Adelaide seaside a Mediterranean look and feel as well as climate. At Henley Beach, where you were lucky to find a feed of fish and chips ten years ago, now the many new eateries are packed out on weekends.

Part of the original city design, North Adelaide remains village-like, the epitome of affluent suburbia. It is an entertainment centre and a good address for sundry professionals. It is also where the wealthy built their villas and mansions.

There is no better place to appreciate the substance and refinement of Adelaide's domestic architecture.

The need to walk to work ensured that the first villages outside the parklands were right on their fringes and in same concern for travelling time and investment meant that Norwood and Unley, especially, benefited from the post-war wave of migration. They, with Hindley Street in the city, became Adelaide's first pockets of cosmopolitanism.

Eating out by the beach

some, such as Parkside, the rediscovery of the convenience and actual pleasure of doing so has been very good for today's property values.

The arrival of horse-drawn trams created the villages of Unley, Mitcham, Norwood, Kensington and Prospect. The

Productive gardens remain a feature of suburban life. Look at some of those villas on their quarter-acre blocks: orange and lemon trees, peaches, apricots and nectarines, a grapevine, a vegetable and herb garden. Chickens are becoming the exception rather than the rule but have not yet been banished entirely to factory cages. In an age of abundant, cheap, packaged food, behind their picket and brushwood fences some of these households are almost self-sufficient. The city has a suburb called Paradise and, nearer town, homes from more than a century of geographic isolation. I once wrote, with a not original but I think apt turn of phrase, that Adelaide was big enough to get lost in but not so big that you feel lost in it.

where people still feed themselves from their tiny Edens.

Adelaide is a metropolis of a million people but it doesn't feel like that. It is very much part of an interdependent, shrunken world but still a city-state that stands on its own with the resilience and personality that come

'The reasons that led me to fix Adelaide where it is I do not expect to be generally understood or calmly judged of at present,' wrote Colonel Light after his plan was unveiled. Later generations have understood, judged and given thanks.

Picnicking in the Adelaide parklands

Suburban back yard in autumn, Hindley Street at night

Norwood Parade, Norton Summit rose garden

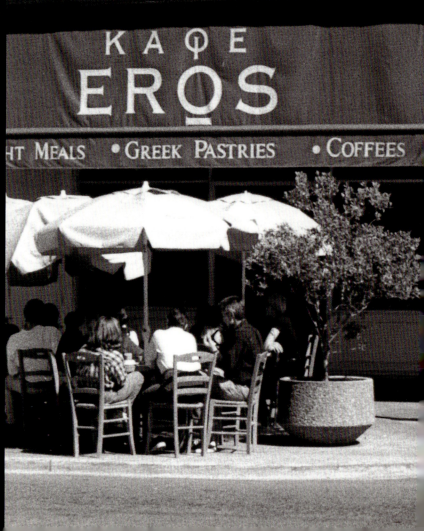

'A place that is vibrant and where you want to be'

Heritage, development, planning and urban design — what works, what doesn't and what still needs to be done — are among Adelaideans' favourite subjects of discussion.

East End | MICK BRADLEY

A 1980s construction boom largely drowned out such talk; cranes spiked the city's skyline as glass and steel rose up from ground level. Then the cranes disappeared and the chatter returned. Now, the criticism is there is too much talk, it's too negative and there is too little action.

Colonel William Light's celebrated town plan for the capital has become the city's backbone, both in shape and psyche.

Governments touch Light's moat of parklands around the city at their peril. Building on the parklands – the 'lungs of Adelaide' – has been equated with San Francisco or Sydney filling in their famous harbours. 'Our parklands are our harbour,' says Adelaide architect Rob Cheesman.

Others, such as University of South Australia urban planning professor Stephen Hamnett, believe that the parklands look tired. Hamnett says that it is time the city relaxed its grip and adopted modern forms of landscaping.

Adelaide's Lord Mayor, Jane Lomax-Smith, is violently opposed to any building on the parklands. 'It is not cheap land – it is priceless land,' she has said repeatedly.

The city's reverence for its past and many of its heritage buildings has led to accusations that parts of Adelaide are anti-development and frightened of modernity; that the community is blind to the need to experiment.

Premier John Olsen served warning on 'the knockers to get out of the way', after howls greeted the news of a major development planned for the city's pedestrian thoroughfare, Rundle Mall.

Lomax-Smith disagrees with the criticism: 'We really do enjoy modern things, but a way to confirm people's timidity is not to offer them good buildings.'

The city's fine Victorian and Edwardian buildings, still to be found on many city streets such as North Terrace and in much of North Adelaide, are its outstanding built asset.

Heritage architect Elizabeth Vines says: 'When visitors come to Adelaide I always take them to the East End. It's no accident that people gather in the East End where there are these delightful buildings. The area is delightful because it has a real sense of cultural history about it.'

Once a commercial precinct dominated by wholesale fruit and produce markets, the East End now flourishes with sophisticated and a youthful nightlife.

'What we've got now is people living around an area which is vibrant and where you want to be,' Vines says. 'People can walk home a few blocks – a much more sensible use of land around the eastern parklands than another lot of empty commercial buildings.'

Debate raged for years over what to do with the former market sites. Some proposed ripping down the heritage buildings and facades to widen footpaths, others suggested high-rises.

Many people in the city want to see the city's nooks and crannies – the laneways and alleys between the bigger streets – turned into inviting places to lose yourself in.

Stephen Hamnett says that developing this 'fine grain' is the key to improving parts of the city. 'By getting more people into certain areas rather than worrying too much about the fronts of buildings – I think that's how you bring about change in cities,' he says.

'The lively bits of cities are always the ones that have small-grade activities. The way we have ruined most Australian cities, including bits of this one, is by losing the fine grain fabric of the mix of uses we used to have. This can only be reversed incrementally over time. We have to stop worrying only about the next big project.'

The most recent debate in Adelaide has been about how to bring people and life back to its heart. Before the Second World War the inner city had a residential population of 40,000. Today less than 12,000 people live there.

The rest of Adelaide, on the other side of the parklands, has sprawled naturally to the north and south, and new regional centres have developed serving these communities. In Marion to the south of the city, for instance, the southern hemisphere's largest cinema complex has been built.

The central business district was ravaged by the recession of the late 1980s and early 1990s. Head offices closed and moved interstate. Public sector 'downsizing' in the mid-1990s contributed to the CBD's problems.

The city's retail market share has dropped from 20 per cent to less than 15 per cent in just over a decade, and forecasts say it could slide further. Despite all this, the inner city remains the largest centre of employment; 75,000

Rundle Street | MICK BRADLEY

Rundle Street MICK BRADLEY

East Terrace MICK BRADLEY

people work in the CBD each day. Housing construction has started in pockets of the city but the overall outcome has been moderate so far.

In many eyes, the city was left to moulder by a stingy city council and ignored by a succession of state governments. Rundle Mall, for example – the first pedestrian mall created in Australia back in 1977 – was hailed at first, but more recently has been derided as the city's black hole. Recent refurbishments are assisting its recovery.

Besides the transformation of the East End, the city's other recent success story has been the development of its precincts.

Until the early 1990s the word 'precinct' was not part of the inner-city vernacular. Now the city and North Adelaide are divided into nine individual precincts. Traders in each corner suddenly realised that they shared a common interest. Battling a reversing economy, they lined up one-by-one at the city council's door, crying for help.

Their precincts, they said, were tired and ugly. Bright lights, fancy seating, flag poles, wider footpaths for outdoor eating and a scattering of public artworks were needed to enliven each area. The city council responded and in turn each precinct established a new identity and designer logo.

One precinct has created more debate than the others combined: the West End and its chief strip, Hindley Street.

This is the inner-city's entertainment and nightlife zone. It is home to tattoo and biker shops, 24-hour bars and strip clubs, as well as a university and bookshops. Urban designers picture Hindley Street with hanging pot plants, palm trees and fancy paving. Debate on whether the sleaze should stay continues.

'Adelaide must choose between relative decline or the challenge of becoming a cosmopolitan, internationally oriented and competitive city,' says Professor of Urban Planning Michael Lennon, who has been leading debate about a new vision for the city.

The Adelaide 21 Report, which surveyed Adelaide's citizens, including the city's opinion leaders, produced a long-term strategy for creating a commercially successful twenty-first-century metropolis characterised by liveliness and style. While capital works projects were at its centre – such as creating pockets of student housing and street-scaping North Terrace – the report's main aim was to build on the city's reputation as a university city and a centre for the arts.

Leading Adelaide urban designer John Bedford sums up the city's strengths: 'With Adelaide's strong tradition of urban design, and as Australia's best-preserved Victorian city centre, we have the creative opportunity to connect the best of the gracious past with a vibrant future.'

Just visiting

It's our Saturday afternoon ritual in summer. Lunch al fresco in Henley Square amid nodding umbrellas, aromas of pasta and coffee and the boisterous sounds of cricket matches drifting up from the beach. That day we watched him busily taking photographs as sunlight struck the white awnings and the cafe fronts, placing light-hearted bets on where he was from.

'Switzerland.' Alison was convinced.

'Canada,' Gina said.

'He's a Pom,' decided Louise.

'Belgium,' someone else said.

Jody, though, said nothing. Instead she got up from our table like a swan rising and went across to him. Within a moment she had engaged him in conversation and led him to our table. Jody is a most impressive woman.

She introduced us one by one and with painstaking good manners we took it in turns to shake his hand. He smiled and nodded at each of us without speaking while Jody sat down again, quietly amused by something.

Then, in the broadest of Australian accents, he said: 'How ya going? The name's Kev.'

The table burst into hilarious laughter, except for Kev. He just looked confused.

'So what's the big joke?'

'We were just taking bets on where you were from,' Alison said.

'Did anyone bet France?'

'France?'

'No,' Gina admitted. 'No one bet France.'

'Too bad. I'm from Paris.'

'Get out of here!'

'It's true. But I grew up here in Henley until I was nineteen. Tell you what, I just about lived out on that jetty in summer. But my mother got a job in Paris eight years ago so we've lived there ever since.'

'We figured only a tourist would wander around here taking photos,' Jody said.

'I wanted to get some shots to take back with me. She won't believe it's the same place.'

'How do you mean?'

'When we lived here this seafront was pretty ordinary. Run down and rusty, you know?'

'We're *far* too young to remember that!' Louise almost sounded convincing.

'Yeah, and I'm Mel Gibson,' Kev said and we laughed. 'But look at it now,' he went on. 'This is fantastic.'

'What's it like, living in Paris?' someone asked.

'It's a hell of a long way to the beach.'

'I'm desperate to see Paris,' Jody said.

'I'm desperate for a coffee,' Kev said without any attempt at subtlety.

Jody bought him one in the blink of an eye.

3 a mosaic

'The ranges consist mainly of sedimentary rocks, though in the north some igneous rocks intrude. It is regarded as being possibly the best display of Precambrian geological formations in the world.'

That encyclopedia description of the Flinders Ranges is only true in the same way as you might say that Rembrandt's works consist of arrangements on canvas of pigments ground in oil.

Instead, as you head into this ancient desert range starting about two hours' drive from Adelaide and extending 430 kilometres, take in the pure, clear light, first of the reasons why the Flinders have captivated painters, photographers and poets. Then you'll begin to understand why they exercise such a hold on the Aboriginal people who are custodians of the Ranges' Dreaming. Look around at the mountains, gorges and chasms, the trees that clothe them and the wildflowers that carpet them after rain. Gaze at those precise shades of every hue of blue and purple, red, orange and brown and dusky olive greens and you will see why the artists return time and again to try to capture the nuances.

Wilpena Pound in the Flinders Ranges | RICHARD HUMPHRYS

Abandoned cottage near Burra | MILTON WORDLEY

South Australia cannot boast any of the 'conventional' natural wonders of the world, no Niagara or Victoria Falls, Grand Canyon or mighty Amazon. Yet travel around the state and you will be treated to a visual feast. Within the Flinders the experiences include Quorn, an old railway town with a steam train that still puffs through Pichi Richi Pass, and Wilpena Pound, a landscape colossus, its ramparts forming a monster hand stretched towards the heavens. The dusty roads and bushwalking trails put you in touch with more than 50 species of birds. Kangaroos, wallabies, euros and emus gather around the deep chasms and quiet waters. Here too are the poignant ruins of settlements that failed for want of water. If you can, watch a sunset and sleep outdoors under stars blazing as you've never seen them before; then a visit to the Flinders becomes a pilgrimage. It is also a journey to the dawn of the earth: the Flinders were once the floor of an ancient ocean and fossil remains of the planet's first animals, the ediacara fauna, have been found there.

I feel the same sense of humility about the Coorong, a flat sand and scrub land finger forming a shallow lagoon that stretches for 145 kilometres from Lake Alexandrina to the fishing ports of the state's south-east. Three kilometres wide at most, the lagoon is protected from the Southern Ocean by the white sandhills of Younghusband Peninsula. It can be eerie in its desolation. The Coorong is never forbidding, though, because this natural sanctuary is home to a

Sunset at the Coorong

multitude of native birds, and is the breeding ground of giant pelicans, ibis, shags, terns and wild duck. Walk the dunes and listen to the cries of the birds and the sound of the rolling surf and the word stress is suddenly meaningless.

The Heysen Trail is the world's longest footpath – 1500 kilometres from its start near Cape Jervis on the tip of Fleurieu Peninsula to its terminus in the Flinders Ranges. The transition of its vistas makes me think that 'On The Heysen Trail' would make a perfect title for a landscape symphony.

In the early 1970s the government of Don Dunstan was at the height of its reformist zeal. In addition to the premiership Dunstan loaded himself with a remarkable number of portfolios, one of which was tourism. As his press secretary I spent a couple of days in Cornwall, birthplace of many of the miners recruited to work the fabulous copper deposits discovered in South Australia in the nineteenth century. In Cornwall we encountered some of the first manifestations of the industrial archaeology movement, which stemmed from the realisation that old factories and mines are as much a part of the national heritage as castles and stately homes.

Back in South Australia at Burra, north-east of Adelaide, this became the right idea for the right place at the right time. Copper had been discovered there in 1845. The mine had a comparatively short life but during its boom

Remarkable Rocks at Kangaroo Island, On the Heysen Trail, Adelaide Hills, Head of the Bight

Eyre Peninsula, Naracoorte Caves, Tarcoola Station in the mid-west, Penong near the west coast

years Burra was home to 1500 people. The buildings of the monster mine had the lean beauty of much functional architecture, as did the local jail. Many of the public and private buildings, including the miners' cottages, were enhanced by

on Yorke Peninsula. While much of what began as commendable regard for history has degenerated into theme-park kitsch with plagues of tourists, these towns radiate innocence.

a creekside setting. Burra today is famous for its merino stud sheep. But it is fair to say that not a lot has happened since the mine closed; the town has been preserved and is locally cherished. Industrial archaeology has helped preserve other former mining towns, especially in the north-east and

Generations of South Australians were convinced that they lived in a place that you left to see the rest of the world. They were genuinely surprised when the tourists started coming here, and for some the novelty still hasn't worn off. The benefits have by no means been confined to dollars, jobs

The Indian Pacific crosses the mighty Nullabor Plain GREAT SOUTHERN RAILWAYS/MILTON WORDLEY

and better amenities. The visitors have made the locals see and appreciate their own splendours, including, for instance, the Naracoorte Caves and Kangaroo Island.

The south-east of the state is a place of pine forests,

truly understand that this was a treasure trove. It has now been formally entered on the world heritage list. The caves are as memorable as the Barrier Reef or Australia's majestic rainforests. Here, over millennia, built up layer upon layer of

vineyards and gum-studded pastures atop a honeycomb of caves. Among these is a network of sixty caves near the small town of Naracoorte. It was probably the state's first tourist attraction – a local publican was organising tours there in 1869. But not until a hundred years later did people

fossils of extinct ice-age animals, such strange creatures as marsupial lions and giant kangaroos. More time travel, South Australian style.

Events rarely work out as planners envisage. When, eventually, South Australians did realise that their state would be a tourist destination there was super-heated talk of planeloads of affluent Americans and Japanese coming to spend their big dollars and yen. Luxury hotels and convention centres were built, the welcome mat laid out. Well, there are such callers, but towards the end of the 1990s the real growth area has been from the backpackers, that new international tribe of nomads, and from eco-tourists, people more interested in the natural world than room service.

These travellers found Kangaroo Island and made South Australians see it themselves. If that is an exaggeration it is only a slight one: it sometimes seems that Australia's third-largest island is as well-known in Dusseldorf and Manchester as in Adelaide. This is one of the world's true wilderness areas, flanked by rugged cliffs and pristine beaches. The island's 18 conservation and national parks safeguard its flora and wildlife, and its lurid past as the refuge of pirates, whalers and villains is barely visible in its patchwork of tidy farms and tiny towns.

A friend once came up with the pretty conceit of a Day Bank. His idea was that you should be able to deposit perfect days just like dollars so that when the black dog threatened you could draw one out of your psychic savings account. It is now nearly twenty years since another friend invited me to spend a day and night messing about on his boat on the Murray River. We drank a glass or three, cruised the tree-lined river and, as evening fell, nudged our way into a

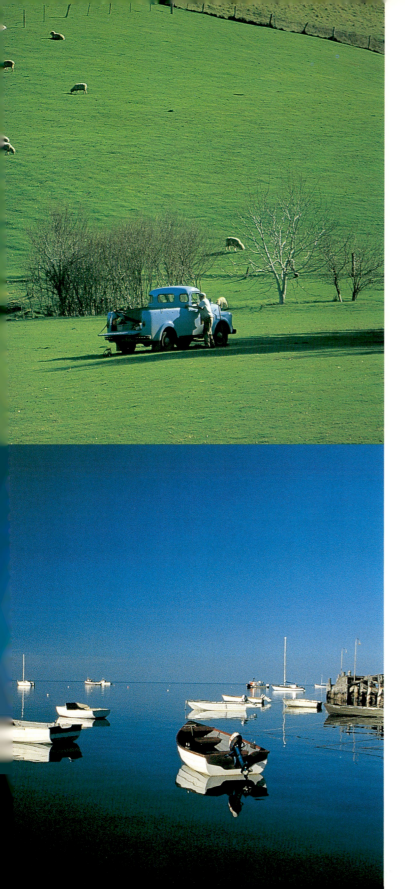

Fleurieu Peninsula farmland

billabong. He caught some carp and we barbecued. Far, far too boney; there was a serpent even in Eden. So we barbecued some meat instead, and enjoyed the stillness of the evening, the scent of meat cooking on the coals of tree roots, the murmured river sounds and the wine made about five kilometres down river. Then the words of Australia's most famous song, Banjo Paterson's 'Waltzing Matilda', came into my head. My God, I realised, I'm camped by a billabong. I still withdraw that day from my memory bank.

The Murray is a focal point in my kaleidoscope of visions splendid. If this book does nothing more than induce people to drive a houseboat and camp by their own billabongs along this great river, the labour will have been worthwhile.

Another such day was spent on another island, one that can make Kangaroo Island seem hectic. Wedge Island, between the great triangle of Eyre Peninsula and the cavalier's boot of Yorke Peninsula, was so named by Matthew Flinders because of its 240-metre limestone cliffs, which confront the Southern Ocean at the entrance to Spencer Gulf. It has been farmland and a wartime radar station but today South Australia's sixth-largest island is being developed as a sanctuary to protect endangered animals and a remote holiday centre. We came in on a half-hour flight from Adelaide, feasted on lobster and whiting, watched black-footed rock wallabies bounding on a clifftop as if dancing to the music of the waves crashing below, and

Kingscote, Kangaroo Island

walked one of the southern state's few north-facing beaches. As we left, determined one day to build the perfect retreat there, we realised that ours were the only human footprints on the beach.

Actually, though, that day we worked quite hard to get away from it all. It is much easier to drive around Yorke Peninsula's boot, 600 kilometres of coastline dotted with tiny ports built for ketches that would take wheat, barley and wool to Adelaide for trans-shipment to the tall ships that raced each other halfway around the world to England.

Yet another perfect day might be spent at Mintaro, the mid-north hamlet a sensible government declared a heritage area in its entirety, famous for its slate and for Martindale Hall, a stately home built by a bachelor for the bride who never arrived.

As visitors from interstate drive into Adelaide across vast dry stretches, the Adelaide Hills come as a multi-coloured surprise. Looking out into the valleys with their variegated plantings of vegetables, vineyards and orchards, you get the sense that this is a land of plenty.

South Australia: politically, legally it is a component state in a sovereign federation. Scenically, it's a mosaic.

'Adelaide could be the wildlife capital of Australia'

Adelaide sits on the rim of the most varied environment to be found in Australia.

'No other Australian capital is so close to so many different habitats,' says Dr John Wamsley, a prominent South Australian environmentalist and tourism operator. 'That gives us all sorts of unfair advantages. Adelaide could be the wildlife capital of Australia.

Yellow-footed rock wallabies in the Flinders Ranges | NICHOLAS BIRKS

'Adelaide is, geographically, ideally placed for this. We have wildlife no one else has. Tourists come to see our wildlife – but not "in vitro". They want to see it in the wild.

'Tourism means a great deal to South Australia and it is extremely important that this state gets it right. We could take people on "safari" to see our wildlife. We could give them an experience they would never forget. We should show them yellow-footed rock wallabies, not sitting on a pile of rocks in a pen in a zoo, but moving across the cliffs like magic doing best what they evolved to do.'

Now that tourism is seen as an essential industry – worth about $2 billion per annum – South Australians are keen to outstrip national tourism growth and encourage those tourists who find their way here to stay longer.

Tourism forecasts say that annual growth figures of 10 per cent for international visitors and two per cent from interstate can be achieved only with better promotion and marketing, more accommodation developments and urban projects and better transport infrastructure. Apart from increasing its profitable conventions trade, South Australia has hitched itself to the major-events bandwagon – including the Australian Golf Open, the Adelaide International Horse Trials, the World Masters Rowing, pre-Olympic training and match practices, and food and wine events such as the hugely successful Tasting Australia.

Eco-tourism is the industry's buzzword. For Wamsley, it is not a fad for the world-weary traveller but virtually a doctrine. 'There are people who are really interested in wildlife just as there are arty people,' he says. The sort of

wildlife Wamsley talks about are the lumbering seals of Kangaroo Island, the numbats of the Murray Mallee, southern right whales in the Great Australian Bight and the yellow-footed rock wallabies – considered the most beautiful of all Australian kangaroos – of the Flinders Ranges.

Wamsley and his wife, Proo Geddes, are devout conservationists. Dedicated to saving Australian wildlife, they

constructed. Rare animals like the bettong, potoroo and pademelon were introduced and thrived, protected by Australia's first dog and cat fence. Wamsley and Geddes established Australia's only successful platypus breeding program.

Warrawong presents wildlife in a habitat not seen since before the white settlement of the Adelaide plain.

have founded a string of sanctuaries across South Australia and have branched out interstate.

They have won several tourism awards including a national environmental tourism honour. They started with

Wamsley has extended Warrawong into Earth Sanctuaries, a company with the declared aim of making protection pay. It seemed to many a quaint idea, until they discovered that the Rothschild investment group had been

Jane Fargher echoes Wamsley's 'wildlife capital' sentiments: 'We have to rethink South Australia, what it is that is so great about it – the fact that we have a relatively unspoilt landscape. It's so vast and raw at the moment. We haven't been over-developed like the eastern states.'

Fargher and her husband Ross live on a pastoral station in the state's mid-north and also own one of South Australia's oldest country hotels, the Prairie Hotel, 35 kilometres away in Parachilna. The central town is an entry point to the Flinders Ranges and the gateway to the outback. It has been a key location for the Opera in the Outback spectacular starring soprano Dame Kiri Te Kanawa. Overnight guests at the Prairie swell Parachilna's official population of seven.

'Nothing else could have brought us that exposure,' says Fargher of international media interest in Opera in the Outback. Shortly afterwards, Adelaide hosted the inaugural Tasting Australia food and wine event and national magazine *Vogue Entertaining* featured the Prairie Hotel's unusual cuisine: Flinders Feral Food.

'It's not enough these days just to have location, no matter how spectacular it is. We decided that South Australia was becoming known for its food and wine and that we needed to do something adventurous, to make the Prairie Hotel more of a package. The inspiration for our menu is the native seasonal produce,' Fargher says. Guests can tuck into kangaroo, emu, omelettes made from emu eggs and pate from emu livers, camel, goat, and saltbush marino lamb. Tuna is brought in from Port Lincoln and oysters from Cowell. There also are plans to develop regional dishes with the local Adnamathyna Aboriginal community.

Fargher says that initiatives like this by small tourism operators need to be rewarded with better exposure. She believes that too much emphasis on large-scale projects with short-term profits will hinder, not help, South Australia's developing tourism industry. 'We have opportunities but we've been slow on the uptake,' she says, adding that this is not necessarily a bad thing. 'We can step back and look at what we can do, not rush into anything, prevent rash, inappropriate decisions with only short-term benefits.' She firmly believes in attracting tourists to stay longer 'rather than concentrating on numbers'.

Petanque at the Prairie Hotel | MILTON WORDLEY

Fargher says past attempts to drive tourism in South Australia have lacked continuity. 'Most people, especially those from overseas, really make an effort to come and see us. These are people with a special interest. And they love it up here. People are often warned in Adelaide that the Flinders Ranges are too hot but it's really only a couple of degrees hotter than Adelaide. It's a different kind of heat, not concentrated like you get in the city,' she says.

The Prairie Hotel attracts interstate visitors and increasing numbers of international tourists, especially European backpackers. One tourist Fargher would rather see less of is the four-wheel driver: 'They make an enormous impact on the environment and provide little economic benefit.

'Some people up here complain that "it's not like the old days", when there were a lot of people and coaches coming through. But who wants to see the gorges flooded with campers? Being in the Flinders Ranges, we can really see where our strengths are but we still need to provide a level of infrastructure so we can bring in the people with money and encourage them to stay here and spend.'

A $6 million tourism development in the Flinders' Wilpena Pound is welcomed by everyone, says Fargher, but she emphasises that pragmatism is called for: 'There need to be some controls, especially over the times and places people can camp. We have to look after what we've got for generations to come.'

Fargher believes tourism in South Australia would be boosted by better links – both transport and promotional – between regions. 'We need more travel options for people who are here for a limited time. People should be able to fly between Kangaroo Island and the Flinders Ranges. It would probably only take two hours. After visiting KI, seeing all its beauty and wildlife and tasting the local produce, travellers should be able to hop on a plane and fly up here for a totally different experience,' she says. 'We have divided our state into regions, now we should be looking more at the big picture. The distances in South Australia are just so great.

'I really think tourism in South Australia is at an exciting stage. With some change in attitudes, we have a healthy future. We just need South Australians to believe in our own product.'

4 the shark and the

South Australia is an ark that got off to an exceptionally bad start. It is customary to portray the modern state as having begun with the arrival of the *Buffalo* and other vessels carrying the founding colonists from faraway Europe. Before the official settlement, though, South Australia was already home to groups of whalers and sealers who hunted these lovely creatures almost to extinction.

Whales were especially prized. Their blubber was used for lamps and soap. Whalebone was sought as stiffening for clothing. To meet the demand, whaling stations were established at Encounter Bay on Fleurieu Peninsula, Sleaford Bay on Eyre Peninsula and Fowlers Bay on the far west coast. Sealers made bases at Kangaroo Island and elsewhere.

A southern right whale – or its tail | SA TOURISM

ark

To modern eyes the spectacle would have been awful and the stench dreadful. The southern right whale was so named by these whalers because it was just right for hunting, being gentle and slow-moving,

A sea lion at Seal Bay, Kangaroo Island

coming close to shore and floating when dead.

This was not the only dimension to what now seem crimes against the environment. South Australians shared the national passion for importing exotic flora and fauna, with calamitous results for the vulnerable native species. Settlers also hunted indigenous wildlife remorselessly.

Against this depressing background there were a few examples of enlightenment. Belair National Park, stretching across the rim of suburban Adelaide into the hills, was established in 1891 as one of the first national parks in the world. This was the birth of a movement that has secured the survival of each of the state's wilderness environments for future generations.

Flinders Chase on Kangaroo Island covers nearly

74,000 hectares and is a haven for the now totally protected sea lions and a profusion of birds.

In the Coorong National Park, a long finger of land and series of lagoons stretching 145 kilometres from the mouth hectares and the Simpson Desert Conservation Park and Regional Reserve in the far north stretches over fully 3.6 million hectares.

Today more than 20 per cent of South Australia is set

of the River Murray to the state's south-east, more than 240 species of native birds have been identified.

Some outback national conservation parks and regional reserves are as big as nation states. Innamincka Regional Reserve in the state's far north-east covers nearly 1.4 million aside for conservation, more than any other mainland state. About 20 million hectares are protected by the state's parks system, and another 500,000 hectares by private landholders through voluntary heritage agreements. The system includes a hierarchy of more than 300 parks covering

Fairy penguins at Penneshaw, Kangaroo Island

Ibis at the Coorong, Kangaroos at Brachina in the Flinders Ranges

Emus near Barmera in the Riverland, Rainbow lorikeets in Adelaide

wilderness protection areas, wetlands such as those at the mouth of the Murray River, world heritage-listed fossil caves, and regional reserves that allow, for example, mining, tourism and conservation to co-exist.

The newest park is a marine park – the Head of the Bight – which protects the breeding ground of southern right whales and sea lions off the west coast where the Nullabor Plain meets the Southern Ocean.

The estimated asset value of this huge parks system and its infrastructure is $2 billion.

The most heartening story of all is that of the whales. The southern rights begin to arrive from Antarctica in May each year. They come to bear and care for their young calves, and are a joy to watch as they surface and hit their tail flukes on the waves. The whales were officially protected in 1935 – by which time the population was down to no more than 200 – but illegal killing is known to have continued at least until 1980. They remain an endangered species facing threats from nets, human harassment, pollution and their much depleted genetic pool. But the seemingly inexorable path towards extinction has been reversed.

Virtue has brought rewards. As whale populations have revived, watching them has become a branch of tourism. Around 10,000 people are now attracted to the Bight's clifftops each year with thousands more streaming out of Adelaide for Victor Harbor to see the whales play in what a century and a half ago were their killing grounds.

More remarkable still is the story of the white pointer or great white shark. The white pointer is the perfect killing machine, with jaw muscles that enable its serrated teeth to punch through metal.

No one had better reason to fear this shark than South Australian diver Rodney Fox, one of the few people ever to survive a white pointer's attack. He owes his life to the creature's habit of mouthing its prey to test its palatability before swallowing it. In one hideous moment Fox literally tore himself from the jaws of death, and even then he nearly died from his wounds. The hunted turned hunter, but as Fox pursued this awesome predator he grew to respect it and lent his weight and prestige to the movement that in 1997 prompted the government to extend limited but meaningful protection to the white pointer.

Fox, who was technical adviser to the movie *Jaws*, now organises trips into the Southern Ocean where people descend in cages to the sharks' world and watch them gorge on meat thrown from the vessel above.

The attitude that today illuminates South Australians' approach to their wildlife was best seen in the case of the Kangaroo Island koalas. When the state was settled in 1836 there were no koalas on the island at all: they were confined to the state's lower south-east corner. By the turn of the century hunting, land clearances, bushfire and disease had depleted the koala population in the south-east. In the 1920s and 1930s conservationists obtained koalas from Victoria and released them in Flinders Chase on Kangaroo Island. The animals found their new home congenial, and the population grew so rapidly that there are now not enough gum trees to feed and maintain them.

The experts recommended a cull. The result would have a public relations nightmare, with an international outcry from wildlife groups, tourism promoters, children and their parents that no amount of explanation could have overcome. Instead, a new marsupial management program has been devised, involving enforced family planning through sterilisation and controlled experiments in removal to mainland homes. While the jury is still out on the effectiveness of these schemes, it is a lot more enlightened than putting a bullet in their brains.

In six generations, the heirs of the whalers have come to realise that they inhabit an ark, have come to cherish it and now seem on the brink of making a profit out of it through eco-tourism and other ventures. By any reckoning that has to be accounted as progress.

Pelicans gather for a feed | ADELAIDE FREELANCE

Frogman

My son is eight.

He stands apart from other boys because he is obsessed by living creatures rather than sport and computer games. He breeds frogs in his bedroom. At school, with a mix of ridicule and respect, they call him the Frogman.

We come here often, just the two of us. We sit and watch and talk as the pelicans and the egrets and the mallard ducks arrive and depart with all the organised chaos of an airport at peak hour.

Recently I tried to convince him that, not very long ago, this place used to be a dump. Not an easy task because when you're twelve it's hard to imagine that the world was ever different.

'No it wasn't a dump,' he decided. 'You're making it up.'

'It *was* a dump.'

'What was here?'

'Nothing,' I said. 'Except mud and bits of old cars.'

'You mean it was like our back yard?'

'Very funny.'

He laughed at my legendary lack of enterprise in the garden and then he asked: 'What lived here?'

'Nothing. And it stank like you wouldn't believe.'

'So how come it got to be like this?'

'People decided to make something better.'

'Yeah? How come?'

'They decided the city should have a back yard with trees and birds and water in it.'

'What sort of people? Scientists and stuff?'

'All sorts. Ideas people, scientists, designers, bird people.'

'Frog breeders?'

'I'm sure there was a frog breeder in there somewhere. Bulldozer drivers, water experts, fish people, tree planters, you name it. They got together and did it.'

For a while he didn't say anything, but I knew he was thinking. He's always thinking. Eventually he said: 'That's pretty cool, Dad.'

'Just shows you, doesn't it?' I said.

'I reckon.'

A pelican swept in silently over our heads, lowered its undercarriage and tip-toed to a splashless landing. We watched it float about fishing for a little while and then Frogman said: 'I've just had a brilliant idea.'

'I was afraid of that,' I said.

'If we got together, we could turn *our* back yard into a wetland.'

What could I say?

'The everyday person actually cares about the environment'

In gumboots and gardening gear, a group of inner-city residents can be spotted most weekends in the parklands that skirt the western edge of Adelaide.

Hi ho, hi ho – Karrendi Primary School students on a water-testing trip in the Salisbury wetlands DON BRICE

Bent over, heads down, they are weeding and planting – greening their adoptive tract of city parklands, which is being gradually transformed with plant life, wetlands and flocking birds. The group includes a passionate founding member in Jane Lomax-Smith, Adelaide's second female Lord Mayor.

Whether it be by the handful, as with this parklands group, or by the hundreds, committed South Australians belong to land care and conservation groups that have befriended creeks, sand dunes, gardens, parks, heritage buildings and homes.

'What's fantastic about this state is the level of community commitment and involvement,' says John Scanlon, chief executive of South Australia's Department of Environment and Natural Resources. 'So many times I hear people say, "I'm really concerned about the environment but I'm not a greenie." Or, "I'm not a greenie but . . ." They are people with legitimate concerns about environmental issues and they are out there in their thousands. Young people, in particular, take quite extraordinary interest in the environment. They have been exposed to the subject through their formal education and through the media.'

More than 6000 volunteers make up the 85 groups caring for South Australia's network of national parks. The Friends of Parks Inc. contributes $5 million annually of in-kind support, the equivalent of about 200 full-time staff. It is the largest Friends scheme in Australia and recently won a national environment award as the country's best green community group.

'Look at the participation in parks and other initiatives like Landcare, Trees For Life, Greening Australia, Water Watch and Coast Care,' Scanlon says. This commitment includes working with outback Aboriginal communities to develop joint management arrangements for individual parks, and helping with biological surveys.

'I think we have an advantage over other states and other parts of the world because we've managed to tap so effectively into the community spirit and people's desire to be involved. We are nowhere near perfect, but I was just reading recently about what the Canadians are trying to do with their national parks – we have a greater level of community involvement. I thought, That's what we've got, we've had it for years.

'We don't have an eco-tourism industry in this state without our national parks,' Scanlon says. However, there are too few caretakers or rangers; many parks are

Adelaide's Lord Mayor with shovel | NAOMI JELLICOE/ADVERTISER

native animal species have been declining, bird life disappearing and native plants becoming rarer.

'One of the problems is how to manage 20 million hectares of parks with a population of just 1.4 million people. What we've done in South Australia is to enlist volunteer support.' The prescription for the future under the $30 million Parks Agenda – a comprehensive plan to protect the park assets – is a partnership both with volunteers (financial support to Friends' groups has doubled) and the corporate sector, through sponsorship and promotion. The latter is viewed with some scepticism by the green movement.

'South Australia has a clean environment and we trade on our green image but there are a number of environmental issues that we need to tackle, and are tackling, and in fact, we are leading Australia and the world in a number of initiatives,' Scanlon says.

Water is the clearest example of how South Australia is translating international policy to action at the community or ground level. 'One of the matters stressed at the Rio Earth Summit in 1992 was that we need to involve the community,' says Scanlon. South Australian legislation that gives individual communities the power to protect and improve their waterway catchment areas 'is a world leader in achieving the Rio aims and has been promoted as a model in South Africa and the Russian federation'. Community-based boards are given their own budgets and certain statutory powers to achieve improvements.

'What brought this to fruition was that our two most prominent metropolitan waterways – the Patawalonga and the Torrens – were heavily polluted and there was a community call for action. You get dirty waterways through dirty catchments and you can only clean up your catchment with the support of local people.

'The beauty of this model is that we are giving the community the opportunity to determine for itself how the catchment ought to be cleaned up. We are also giving it the resources to achieve that clean-up and implement physical change through the development of wetlands, trash racks, and all sorts of management practices.'

Before his appointment as the state government's environment chief – the youngest in the country – Scanlon was an environmental lawyer involved in exporting South Australian environmental expertise. He worked both solo and in partnership with other Adelaide lawyers on several

A Karrendi Primary School student trudges the wetlands DON BRICE

Friends of Mount George Conservation Park DON BRICE

World Bank-funded projects, particularly in the Russian federation. 'There was huge interest in Russia in what we'd done with catchment management,' he says, adding that there is great potential for South Australia to export more of its environmental knowledge. 'We are only just starting to realise that what we know and what we've done is valuable to other parts of the world.' South Australia has a history of 'novel and interesting' environment initiatives that include a recoverable levy on drink bottles and cans – 'an early use of an economic instrument to achieve environmental improvement' – and a permit system to control the clearing of native vegetation in rural areas. Scanlon says that the state's Native Vegetation Act has been hailed internationally and recognised as being peculiarly South Australian.

Among the state's potential exports is its 'world's best environmental legislation', which has already been copied by several other Australian states. 'Essentially, we are focusing on pollution prevention – not prosecution – and what we can do to reduce pollution produced at source. Our legislative model includes all sorts of innovative techniques, such as environmental improvement programs that are negotiated with industry.' Companies are given time-frames in which to improve their operations, without fear of closure and job losses. Scanlon, however, acknowledges that the wider community has been frustrated and often bewildered

Heathfield Primary School students clean up Glenelg beach

injecting it into aquifers, so you can make use of it in summer.'

Scanlon's personal challenge is to 'mainstream the environment'. 'Move it away from being an "add-on" to the agenda; show that the environment is part of the whole equation. Your everyday person is actually interested, and cares greatly about the environment. When I started doing environmental law back in 1984, people would say, "What are you doing that for?" Ten years later I had people phoning me up: "How did you get into that?" Now, we've got masters' courses in environmental law, we've got an Environmental Defender's Office. I think we are recognising that we've got to stop putting so much effort into strategies. It's time to get on and do some effective work on the ground.'

by what seems to be a lenient attitude towards polluters. He says that the range of fines for breaching agreements needs to be amended.

Apart from improving the national parks and eliminating feral animals, Scanlon says that the environmental challenges facing South Australia are solving the problems of land degradation and erosion, salinity levels in the state's chief water source, the Murray River, and water catchment management. 'Adelaide discharges as much stormwater into the ocean as its population uses in a year. That's not smart. What we are starting to do is collect it, treat it in wetlands and at the same time look at storing it and

Tennyson Dunecare members mending fence-posts

creative energy 2

cuisine of the

For first course, yabbies with a lentil salad and tomato and coriander salsa; as the main dish, a kangaroo pie, the meat generously anointed with claret and port; to finish, lemon myrtle bavarois with rosella flower jelly or pot roasted quinces. Those are just three of the scores of dishes with an Australian accent created in and around Adelaide in the past year or so.

But South Australia produces such great food that there is no need to cook it at all. All you need to do with a Kangaroo Island brie is slice it. With an apple from Norton Summit in the Adelaide Hills, just bite.

Woodside Cheesewrights' Edith goat's cheese sandwiched between Kangaroo Island Pure's brie and camembert | TOBY RICHARDSON

Let's begin this unending feast with a look at the creation of the new Australian cuisine.

It *is* new. The emergence of multicultural Australia introduced Australians to the ethnic foods of the Mediterranean, the Aegean and the Levant. Already familiar with Asian cooking, though in the debased form of take-away sweet'n'sour Chinese, we enthusiastically embraced Thai and other spice-is-nice Asian cuisines and French nouvelle cuisine. But it took the combination of a better-educated, more widely travelled population, a dazzling range of local ingredients and the passion of a generation of creative cooks to forge all this into a new cuisine of the southern sun.

South Australia cannot and should not try to claim any monopoly. But, because of some of those chefs and with the additional stimulus of its strong wine industry – a target audience of gourmets and tooth merchants if ever there was one – the state has been in the vanguard. It is no coincidence that one of the nation's most creative restaurateurs, Maggie Beer, started with a ground-breaking restaurant in the premier wine region, the Barossa.

Since what has been called fusion food is a symphony of French, regional Italian and pan-Asian zapped with Californian cool, it also seems only proper than another of the originators, Cheong Liew, came to Adelaide from Kuala Lumpur.

Andrew Fielke is another to stand out. He trained as a chef in Adelaide, made the obligatory pilgrimage to Europe then returned home and joined the gathering movement to use native produce such as yabbies and marrons (crustaceans), kangaroo, emu, buffalo, crocodile and, for the less adventurous, saltbush mutton. This has made his Red Ochre restaurant in the city a shrine for visitors, who there encounter such tastes as muntries, kurrajong seeds, quandongs, warrigal greens and bush tomatoes.

In a sense, there was nothing new about these adventures. Aboriginal Australians knew how fertile the land was thousands of years ago. European and later Asian migrants chose to turn their backs on it. But it says much about our times – and perhaps our common sense – that in one bound kangaroo has gone from pet food to gourmet experience.

It is often said that Adelaide has more restaurants or restaurant tables than any other Australian city. I have never been able to find the basis of that calculation but, after writing about restaurants continuously for nearly twenty years, I can assert that we are home to some of the best and cheapest. On any lifestyle balance-sheet the fact that your restaurant bill will be twenty to fifty per cent lower than at a comparable establishment on the eastern seaboard has to be a credit entry.

Among the 700-odd restaurants in and around Adelaide, many of them Mediterranean-influenced venues offering outside dining, there are places of stellar quality. And there is wonderful variety: you can eat African,

Argentinian, Chinese, English, French, Greek, Indian, Italian, Japanese, Korean, Malaysian, Mexican, Middle Eastern, modern Australian, Russian, Spanish, Swiss, Thai, Ukrainian or Vietnamese as the mood suits. Wine bars and noodle bars are mushrooming, and vegetarians catered for. Many city, suburban, hills and country hotels have transformed their dowdy dining rooms into decent restaurants.

Any chef worth her skillet or his wok will tell you that it has to start on the farm, in the orchard, the grove, the market garden or the waters. Here South Australia is well favoured. Although the climate can be generalised as Mediterranean, local variations shift from the cool, sometimes near-alpine winters of the Adelaide Hills to the sun-drenched summers of the Riverland and further north. This is why the apples are as good as the oranges, the pears the match of the peaches.

As domestic and export demand have gathered strength a variety of producers have begun to take advantage of regional climates and quirks. Kangaroo Island is becoming a producer of a variety of gourmet foods. Its pure-bred Ligurian bee honey is a by-word and so, thanks to the absence of predators, are its free-range chickens. Olive growers are pressing south of Adelaide at McLaren Vale, north on the Adelaide Plains and elsewhere. Some of the most exquisite smoked salmon in Australia is processed in the Adelaide Hills, where market gardeners grow multiple

Fresh today at the Central Market | ADAM BRUZZONE

varieties of potatoes as well as exotic greens for Asian homes and restaurants.

The natural harvest of South Australia's pure ocean waters – King George whiting, snapper, garfish, lobster, abalone, tuna, scallops, mussels, squid and octopus – has been keenly appreciated since the first net was cast. Fishing folk have developed lucrative export markets in Asia and America. Nature these days is given a nudge with oyster and tuna farms along the west coast. Trout and yabbies are farmed in inland fresh waters, barramundi and other fish on the coast.

Visitors are sometimes surprised by the quality of what is on offer in South Australia. Not least, this is because the producers here are rarely self-obsessed or precious. They are breezy and matey, and it takes a while to realise that they are also expert and dedicated. I still cherish the sight of a T-shirt in the north of the state emblazoned with the slogan 'Eat beef, you bastards'. Every time I read of some multi-million dollar quango-initiated promotion campaign I think of that and am reassured.

Mention has already been made of the Central Market behind the Adelaide Hilton just off Victoria Square. It should be a great shout. Said to be the oldest city market in one location in Australia, it is one of Adelaide's jewels. For a gourmet lunch, take a few dollars and walk the market nibbling – a loaf or roll here, slice of salami, chunk of cheese there, a piece of fruit, handful of nuts or olives. One of the nation's top food writers, Barbara Santich, produced a food guide to Adelaide called *Apples to Zampone*. The latter is a pork-based Italian speciality produced by a butcher fronting the central market. A to Z, enough said.

Back in 1984 a group of winemakers in the Clare Valley, about two hours' drive north of Adelaide, had an idea based on a moveable feast or progressive picnic. Each winery would twin for a day or two with a local or city restaurant. The chef would provide a starter-size plate of food, the winery a glass of red or white. People would have one of each, then move on to the next place. A good-time, value-for-money outing. The idea then spread to the Barossa, where they have turned it into an entire gourmet weekend, with music as well. Then it was McLaren Vale, and now South Australia has food festivals the way other places have football matches. That's another of the pleasures that keep me here. I am partial to any city where you can visit six restaurants and sample six fine wines in a single day. (I regard the music as optional.)

In my next chapter I take a loving look at the product that makes people smile when they hear the words South Australia. I predict that before the next century is very old the state's branded, high-quality foodstuffs will have the same international impact as its wines.

'A lot of people are coming to South Australia for food experiences'

For a city that is supposed to have long pockets when it comes to dining out, Adelaide never seems to have trouble spending inside its Central Market.

Pick an entrance, wander in, especially on a Saturday morning, and the aisles will be crammed with baskets, bags and trolleys overflowing with fresh produce and tonight's dinner.

Adelaide Central Market – spot the sack of potatoes

STEVEN MORENOS

Beneath the shouts of the stallholders can be detected the sound of stomachs rumbling. The most inhibited eater becomes brazen in the Central Market.

Juicy Kalamata olives and fetta cheese nestle alongside

'I think South Australia should be very proud of the Central Market. It's the only one like it in the centre of an Australian city; it's got fantastic character,' says Adelaide master chef Cheong Liew.

Polish sausages and Hungarian salamis, bok choy bunches and chilli, local roma tomatoes, Streaky Bay oysters and garfish from the gulf waters, sushi and rollmops, fresh pasta, organic potatoes, wood-oven baked bread and goats' cheese trucked down from the Adelaide Hills.

Cheong – as he is simply known by everyone – is one of the market's best customers. He wanders just a few paces into the bustle from his kitchen at Adelaide's international Hilton Hotel and can often be spotted returning with some morsel that caught his eye.

'It is common for South Australian chefs to go out and scout for their own produce. Most eastern states people are amazed by the Central Market. You have to drive round half of Melbourne to get one ingredient. Sydney chefs don't Valley restaurateur turned gourmet producer, famous for making pheasants into pate, says South Australia has 'developed a strong food culture here for so long because we were lucky enough to have such a multicultural society'.

know where to go and shop. They've got a system, they use a food broker – for fruit, veg, meat, fish, everything. You have to trust the broker.' Cheong says.

Under the barn-like roof of the market is Adelaide's contribution to the global village. Maggie Beer, Barossa

She gives the credit for the progress of the local food culture to the free settlers and German immigrants in the nineteenth century, the Greeks and Italians after the Second World War and the tone set by premier Don Dunstan in the 1960s and 1970s. 'When Dunstan called Adelaide "the

Torrens Island fish market near Port Adelaide

Athens of the South", a pile of people were drawn into that vision. It's often said that proportionally there's more food grown and more that comes out of South Australia than anywhere else.'

Beer has become a niche exporter herself, sending 400 pots of pate as well as quince paste and verjuice (secondary grape juice) to Japan each fortnight. Europe is next in her sights. Awarded the top honour for an Australian business woman, she is a culinary ambassador for South Australia but particularly her beloved Barossa Valley: 'It is truly a region because as well as the regional food and the wine we also have the culture.

'People are hungry for the "story" of where things come from. It means a lot that food came from the Barossa. It matters that it came from South Australia with its clean, green image. There is identity, there is tradition, there is excellence.'

Despite Adelaide's isolation and jibes at its provinciality, the city is undoubtedly a culinary focus in Australia, Cheong says, while Beer believes the state is in the midst of a restaurant resurgence that is being noticed nationally and internationally. 'A lot of people are coming to Adelaide or South Australia for food and wine experiences.'

Cheong agrees: 'Adelaide is absolutely spoilt at the moment. I would like to take visitors on a food tour of Adelaide. It would be one of the best food tours in the world,

and the prices are ridiculously cheap.

Peer into most Adelaide restaurants on, say, Tuesday night, and chances are they will be far from full, yet it will be hard to find a main course over fifteen dollars. It is almost fashionable to sneer at this cheap and empty image. Cheong views Adelaide's quietness as creative free space.

'Adelaide is a place where you have the freedom to express yourself and cook anything you like. In bigger cities no one would dare try anything new because they are having to cope with the demand of people coming in every night.

'So many people who come from eastern states to work say that Adelaideans are a bit more demanding when it comes to quality and price.

'You really have to work harder here. If someone were to open a normal restaurant and think, "I can just do what is good enough to run a restaurant," they will never succeed.

'The eastern states make their restaurants beautiful. We have to be exceptionally good in our work. I don't think Adelaideans care so much about the decor, as long as they get what they want.'

The importance of the Regency Park hospitality and hotel management school cannot be overlooked. Cheong closed his famous Neddy's restaurant in Adelaide to join the northern suburbs hospitality school in the 1980s. He

says that the school's tuition in the fundamentals of cookery, combined with ethnic influences and training restaurants, have produced young chefs 'with more information on products, ingredients and cooking techniques than any other chefs around the world' and set benchmarks for the rest of the country.

'Here the chefs are willing to share their information outright. This state has a sense of the chef's individuality, whereas interstate once a restaurant has this new dish everybody's got to have it. Everybody here is trying to create an individual style.'

Beer agrees: 'I think we are an incredibly creative state. You don't have to copy everyone else if you are creative. We are more isolated as well, which is good in many ways. You don't follow trends. We are also more produce-driven in South Australia.'

South Australia, more than any other state, 'eats from its own back yard'. Almost all the seafood consumed on local tables, for example, comes from the waters off the state's coast. 'Even the little shops sell good quality fruit and veg,' Cheong says, still displaying some amazement after living in Adelaide for nearly two decades.

Beer puts Adelaide's discerning tastes down to distance and climate. 'Our markets are so accessible, and the farmers are so accessible to markets, that we have very good produce easily available. Our Mediterranean climate gives us, for instance, the greatest tomatoes in Australia. In lots of ways we've been spoilt, but that's great.'

Both predict that Kangaroo Island will become the state's larder. Normally noted for its wilderness landscapes, Kangaroo Island has a 'pure clean environment. It's a virgin island and is going to be the best spot for a lot of food,' Cheong says. Kangaroo Island already produces chicken, lamb, seafood, honey and cheese.

'The lamb we get from there, compared to other lamb, has a sweet flavour. It's the salt air, the saltbush leaves, the gentleness of the water they're drinking. The lamb is beautiful and creamy,' Cheong says.

Beer is in raptures about the 'amazing marron, the island's chicken and oysters. It has great pasture, it's so pristine, it's the state's food bowl. There are incredible opportunities but it's going to be about getting products across to the mainland. That's a financial disincentive.'

Food production and exports have the potential to follow the inspirational path set by wine as a major industry for South Australia, Beer believes. The key is to match the innovative streak the farmers already possess with a passion for their products. A recent example of this is the development of the local olive oil industry.

'There is nothing like farmers who are passionate about their food. They want it to taste better, because they love eating it,' Beer says. 'It's such a simple equation. But so many farmers only see it from the point of view of sending produce off the farm and not what the end product can give them. South Australia is big enough to make a difference and small enough to pull together. We haven't the cultural traditions but we haven't been contained by boundaries.'

Beer believes that South Australia's future as a food exporter depends on more niche producers breaking into international markets and 'giving us an image of excellence'. However, there are huge difficulties and barriers for small businesses wishing to export, such as high quarantine fees no matter how much of a product is exported. 'It's the small people who are driven and passionate and can fly straight to the top of the tree. They're the people who will brand South Australia as being incredible.

'If everyone in Australia understood every part of the food chain and respected it, how wonderfully well-off our lives would be. That's my dream. We should live to eat, not eat to live.'

6 The wines of

The approach road to Seppeltsfield in the Barossa is lined with stately palm trees, sentinels planted as a work project during the depression years. It dips into a lush valley on either side of a creek. There, amid manicured gardens, is the castellated Seppelt winery, built by one of the founding fathers in another of those extraordinary flights of ambition that are the hallmark of South Australia's formative years.

In another imaginative move the first Seppelts decreed that each year they would retain a barrel of their best port. This means that Seppelt is the only winery I know that since 1978 has been able to offer bottles of century-old vintage port. It is more than a curiosity, this wine. The olive green of very old port has darkened further to almost the colour and thickness of sump oil. The flavours are heady, complex and make a cathedral of your mouth, lingering as scent and aftertaste long afterwards.

Nearby at the Penfolds winery – also now owned by the same prosaically named Southcorp company – they make Australia's most famous red, Grange, and cellar it for five years before release. This is a shiraz so powerful that it can seem a pup after twenty years.

Although the years can do to wine what alchemists sought to do to base metals, age doesn't always matter, as anyone who has tasted a glass of young South Australian riesling or sauvignon blanc will testify. South Australia supplies all tastes.

Wine has been part of the scene from the outset. The first vines were planted in 1837. A vineyard was established at Reynella, south of the city, by 1839. The first commercial Barossa planting was in 1847. In 1845 Walter Duffield sent Queen Victoria a case of his hock vintaged in the Adelaide Hills. It is not recorded whether she was amused by his presumption.

The industry was already flourishing when the phylloxera louse devastated Victoria, the biggest Australian producer and exporter, from 1875 onwards. By rigorous quarantine measures and shrewd marketing, South Australian vignerons seized the advantage and today they account for half the Australian production.

It is a tapestry of an industry. Four major producers, Southcorp, Orlando Wyndham, BRL Hardy and Mildara Blass are responsible for eighty per cent of total production. But within South Australia's borders there are 222 wineries scattered around ten regions, many of them small or family concerns. Ownership covers the spectrum from multi-national, public and private companies, partnerships and even, at Clare, the Jesuit order. (At Willunga there is a high school that teaches winemaking!) Production is rising to a projected 412 million litres by the end of the century. This works out at 392 bottles a year for every man, woman and child in the state.

These days the wine is most likely to be table wine, red preferred overall to white and with an increasing preference for bottled wine rather than casks. The fortified wines that were once the mainstay of the industry have become a small segment, about a tenth of the unfortified market.

Producers can honestly claim to make the best as well as the most. South Australian wines stand out on the Australian capital city show circuit each year with the highest tally of trophies and medals. They have had similar success at international competitions in Europe and America.

The most sincere measure of all has been soaring export success. This is because South Australian winemakers have become the most technologically sophisticated in the world to the extent they have been contracted, hired outright or embarked on their own ventures to work similar wonders in such traditional wine countries as France and Italy as well as eastern Europe, the United States and South America.

They have mastered (a verb which prompts me to add

that an increasing number of leading winemakers are women) the problems of a hot summer vintage. Cool fermentation and use of precision equipment to eliminate or minimise oxidation have bestowed on the finished wines today's dollars, by 2025. (To keep this in perspective, that would still equate to only 3.25 per cent of the world wine market.) The state produces the most successful Australian wine ever, Orlando's Jacob's Creek, top seller nationally,

McLaren Vale vista

freshness and burst-in-the-mouth fruit flavours. With reds, judicious use of oak and blending have resulted in wines that are softly, beguilingly drinkable in their youth.

The rewards are considerable. South Australia is looking to a $2.25 billion production, wholesale and in exported to every inhabited continent. To cope with the demand the winery in the Barossa has a crushing capacity of 30,000 tonnes, storage capacity of 72 million litres and its bottling facilities can produce 39,000 bottles an hour.

The return from wine export is not limited to the direct

input on the balance of payments. Few, if any, products have done more to proclaim to the rest of the world that Australia can be synonymous with excellence and expertise. Each bottle is an ambassador. Wine is the state's and the nation's

benign. The man-made landscapes of green vineyards against the sunburnt fawns of the Australian summer – and with the gnarled, brown, naked vines and green backdrop of winter – are almost voluptuous in their

flagship export. It is also a branch of the tourism industry. Most of South Australia's wineries have hospitable cellar doors and each region stages its own festival. The biennial Barossa Vintage Festival celebrated its fiftieth year in 1997.

Unlike so many industries, wine is environmentally

visual impact and they are as varied as the state itself.

Colonel Light named the Barossa (with a later mild misspelling) after a place near Jerez in Spain where he had fought. The red soil vistas and bleached gold of the folded hills he first saw in summer must have jogged his memory.

The Barossa wines were pioneered by a mixture of Lutheran Germans and English settlers. Their descendants are among the leaders six generations later. This is the home of majors Orlando and Blass as well as Seppelt and Penfolds, together with boutiques of charm and quality. You can see tradition in the vineyards as well as the buildings, with some vines grown on bushes rather than trellises.

An hour's drive further north, the Clare Valley is a mixture of dairy and wine country, its vineyards planted on rolling pastures with huge patches of purple Salvation Jane, a weed but an exceptionally pretty one. The Clare's dry rieslings are among the best of a wine style that Australia has made its own.

After a gap of more than a century the Adelaide Hills are again criss-crossed with vineyards, some on precipitous hillsides. South Australia has produced a number of winemakers who, in terms of innovation and the sheer pleasure they have given to so many people, can be called great. The late Max Schubert created Grange for Penfolds, in the face of fierce opposition. The ebullient German migrant Wolf Blass brought a touch of genius to the creation of reds that are lip-smackingly accessible while young but have staying power for a decade or more. A third winemaker, Brian Croser, led the flavour revolution into its next phase. He had the foresight to see the potential of the Adelaide Hills, especially for sparkling wine, and the drive to make it happen.

The vineyard John Reynell planted at Reynella is now

Pinot noir grapes at the Henschke vineyard in the Adelaide Hills | M.WORLEY

The seasons of the sun in South Australian vineyards

Riverland, Adelaide Hills, Southern Vales, Coonawarra

surrounded by suburbia, but Australia's oldest continuing winery is still the pride of the McLaren Vale wineries strung along the coast between the southern Mount Lofty Ranges and the sea. Originally celebrated for rich ports and earthy high-alcohol reds, McLaren Vale is now better known for more well-balanced reds and complex whites such as buttery chardonnays. Some 60 wineries, most of them small, make this the state's wine coast.

A four-hour drive south-east of Adelaide brings you to Padthaway. Once pastoral country, it was planted with vineyards in 1963. Now that the vines have come to maturity Padthaway is producing some of the most sought-after wines in Australia.

The development of Padthaway was a demonstration that this is still a land of frontiers. Near Bordertown on the Victorian border, and Robe in the south-east, new wine regions are being nurtured, with others, as yet unidentified, almost certain to follow.

An hour further on from Padthaway is the Coonawarra. This is startlingly flat land for wine country, but part of it is a long geological freak of terra rossa red soil which is perfect for grape growing. The Coonawarra wines have been likened to those of Bordeaux and the Cote d'Or in Burgundy in their finesse, the drinking equivalent of the steel fist in the velvet glove.

The biggest surprise of all is provided by the Riverland along the River Murray. This is the major part of the lands

Bringing in the grapes at Charles Melton's in the Barossa | ADAM BRUZZONE stretching into Victoria and New South Wales that provide the bulk of Australian wine. The word 'bulk' is appropriate in a quantity sense only. By picking grapes at night and using ultra-modern techniques and machinery, winemakers in this area have been the spearhead of a wine revolution.

On any one day there will be more than 8000 different wines available around Australia, 4000 of them from South Australia. It is a happy thought.

Even then, the story is not complete. In an era of big business brewing, Adelaide retains one of the world's nicest boutique breweries. Cooper's is tucked away in the improbably posh suburb of Leabrook. Its grand products include a meaty stout and what has become a cult ale among Australian and overseas beer fanciers. Cooper's Sparkling Ale has an almost chewy consistency and its appearance in the glass gave birth to the memorable meteorological slogan 'Cloudy But Fine'.

Then in 1993 Duncan MacGillivray fermented surplus lemons from a neighbour's orchard. He called the world's first alcoholic lemonade 'Two Dogs' after a joke that regretfully we cannot print here. This new entrant to the ranks of so-called alcopops was regarded as a drop of refreshing whimsy until South Australians woke up one day to discover that Two Dogs had been taken over by the French-based Pernod Ricard group.

Whatever next? It is not an exclamation but an intriguing question.

Barossa Valley scene

'With wine, we haven't even begun to do what we can do'

For a community that taught itself to drink wine out of a box – 'Chateau Cardboard' as it was dubbed in the 1970s – South Australians easily discuss the merits of wooded versus unwooded chardonnay.

New winemaker Caroline Dunn at the Mildara Blass winery in the Barossa Valley RICHARD HUMPHRYS

South Australians are not a bunch of wine snobs but they are quite parochial about the home-grown product. Their general wine knowledge reflects the status that wine has attained in the last two decades. Not surprisingly, Adelaide is the location for a proposed national wine centre.

Wine, above all else, permeates the state's economic, cultural, historical and social layers. South Australia has always thought of itself as Australia's wine state, and bragged about it. Now it shouts the message.

Australia's first Master of Wine – one of the highest qualifications in the world of wine involving rigorous study and examination – was a South Australian.

He is Michael Hill-Smith, who appraises the State's wine industry from his swanky bar, restaurant, wine school and wine shop, the Universal Wine Bar in the city's East End.

Besides his Master of Wine, Hill-Smith also has credits for wine consulting, judging, writing, broadcasting and, of course, producing.

Descended from a long line of wine-makers, Hill-Smith sold his equity in Yalumba, a large South Australian wine company, and formed Shaw and Smith, one of the small wineries that have recently started on the slopes of the Adelaide Hills.

'Wine is very much the product of the here and now. In a state where we struggle to find real export success, wine is a winner for South Australia,' Hill-Smith says.

'Take anyone from anywhere in the world and walk down Gouger Street or Rundle Street on a summery Sunday evening. You've got that sea of tables, everyone eating outside, and there's wonderful food representing all different cultures. And everyone's drinking wine. It's buzzy, it's exciting, it's really unusual. "Let's get out a corkscrew and open a bottle" – that's very much a South Australian approach.'

Wine is a winner and everyone – especially governments – loves being associated with a winner.

Yet twenty years ago, people like Hill-Smith were knocking on doors, trying to develop export markets with little help. The Australian Wine Centre in London was sandwiched between a sex shop and a coffee house in Soho.

Meanwhile, back at home, South Australia was ripping out hectares of vines. The government-sponsored vine-pull

varieties. The sadness is that some old shiraz and grenache vines were pulled out that now would have been very much in demand,' Hill-Smith says.

'We've gone some way to rectify that. In the last few years there has been some really significant planting of premium and super-premium grapes everywhere. But we need more.'

Jacob's Creek, a blend from the Barossa, became Britain's most popular red wine, opening doors for other labels. North America has started to take notice, while Hill-Smith says the potential of the Asian market is 'extraordinary'.

'The British trade realised that Australia is producing wines of tremendous flavour and value,' he says.

The reality of all this success, notes Australian wine authority Len Evans, is that the Australian wine industry produces just two per cent of the world's wine; South Australia's share is even less than that.

One winery in California produces the equivalent – but not the quality – of the whole of Australia's output. Hill-Smith says: 'Given all the success we've had, all the column inches that have been written, all the exposure, all double the size of the Australian and South Australian wine industry in ten years, we may as well stay boutique winemakers.

'That's why I get really angry when I read people saying,"Oh, we're planting too many vineyards, we're setting ourselves up for a big fall, we're going to have another vine-pull scheme." All that stuff is just nonsense. I just don't think everyone quite understands what the wine industry can be.

'There's a huge amount of undeveloped land in South Australia at relatively cheap prices that has terrific potential. The Adelaide Hills and Mount Gambier are two new areas.

'Len Evans says, and I agree with him, that Australia, and South Australia, can become one of the most significant wine producers in the world. That means as important as France and Italy. We haven't even begun to do what we can do.'

Given the potential of South Australia's wine regions, Hill-Smith says that no one should be left behind. 'There are a hell of a lot of small makers who want to be a part of it, and

Checking the quality | RICHARD HUMPHRYS

there are probably a hell of a lot who don't get a great return on their investment, but they are in it for the lifestyle and other reasons. Everyone can share. What may happen is that as more grapes are planted the prices will come down to a saner level.'

Twenty years ago when Hill-Smith started sipping,

swishing and spitting as a wine judge, the wine was often rough and unready. 'You found a lot of technical problems, a lot of faulty wine. And there was a very limited choice. There was riesling and shiraz, but there were no pinots, no chardonnays. The strength of the local industry is that it has continually improved itself.'

Just about everyone in the South Australian industry has had some sort of formal training. The state has been exporting wine technology for several years, especially to the French. South Australian viticulturists understand about sanitation, juice handling and protecting clean water supplies, vital in the state with Australia's lowest rainfall.

Regionalism is on the rise. Wine areas are clearly defining their boundaries in order to cultivate a distinct district identity. But the industry is careful not to overplay wine's 'snob appeal', as evidenced by the popular regional food and wine festivals.

'Wine needs to be fun, tied in with food. The festivals show that South Australia has this relaxed, knowledgeable – but not too serious – approach to wine. It's been a useful way of promoting the industry,' Hill-Smith says.

Wineries also are looking at adding attractions, such as restaurants and museums, for visitors venturing out on the local wine trail.

Historically, South Australian wineries have produced an entire range: from sparkling wines to reds, whites and

Sulphur dioxide analysis | RICHARD HUMPHRYS

fortified. They are no longer afraid of becoming more focused.

'I think people are starting to understand they'll do far better if they think, What does the Clare do best? What does the Coonawarra do best?' Hill-Smith says. 'If we are going to fulfil our potential, we have to understand what areas produce the best grapes and try not to cover all the bases.'

The Barossa, for example, should concentrate on shiraz,

he says, the Clare on riesling and shiraz. Eden Valley makes outstanding riesling, shiraz and cabernet; the Coonawarra's famed terra rossa soil is perfect for its cabernet sauvignon. Sparkling wines, sauvignon blanc, pinot noir and chardonnay flourish in the crisp Adelaide Hills.

'Before, winemakers did really see themselves as selling primarily in a local market. There isn't a winemaker now who isn't aware of selling internationally,' Hill-Smith says.

'The wine politics, the wine bureaucracy – they're all set up. There are good mechanisms for export. The most important thing is a sense of belief, a shared vision about what can be achieved. That's what's really going to make it happen.'

The cyclist

She swears it happened exactly like this.

She was cycling along a glaring white limestone track in the Bordeaux region of France, somewhere between the villages of Lussac and Puisseguin. The heat was already wrinkling the air above the vines.

She came upon two men shouting at each other in French. They didn't notice her approaching or that they were blocking her way so she stopped a little distance off.

There was something vaguely familiar about the younger of these men and after a brief moment she realised what it was. He was Australian. He was speaking French the way she spoke it herself, with a struggling nasal flatness. His anger made the struggle all the more apparent.

Suddenly the other man gave a contemptuous shrug and strode off. The Australian, sensing her presence, glanced around.

'*Excuse mou, mademoiselle*,' he apologised.

'That's all right,' she said in English.

He stared at her. 'Australian?'

'*Oui, monsieur*.' She thought he had an interesting face. 'What was that all about?'

'I've made him extremely unhappy. Told him he has to change the way he does things or his winery will go out of business before he knows it.'

Then she made a fool of herself. 'I thought over here you'd be working for him,' she said.

His eyes hardened. 'Yes, well you would think that. They obviously don't make wine where you come from.'

Embarrassed, she made her admission: 'I'm from South Australia actually.'

'That makes it even worse.'

Instinct told her that this man was about to spoil her day. 'Whatever your problem is, don't take it out on me thank you very much.'

For a few seconds they sized each other up there between the vineyards. Then he attempted to explain. 'We used to come over here to see how it was done. These days, though, they sometimes invite us South Australian winemakers over to show them how we do it. Mostly they take notice,' he added with a smile. 'You wouldn't like a nicely rounded merlot by any chance?'

'It's ten o'clock in the morning and I don't particularly want to have a merlot, nicely rounded or otherwise, with someone who's rude.'

He grinned stupidly at her. 'This isn't going well, is it? Perhaps we should start again.'

She relates this story to their friends whenever she uncorks a bottle of his prize-winning red. He's quick to dismiss it as an unfair distortion of the way he behaved on the day they met. Sometimes though, when he's working alone in their vineyard under the sun, he wonders what might have become of him if she'd ridden away.

RICHARD HUMPHRYS

7 a festive

The Adelaide of 1960 would horrify its present citizens. Governed by its austere, teetotal premier, Sir Thomas Playford, it was a puritan city-state.

The pubs closed at six and daring sophisticates could not order wine after eight in such restaurants as existed. There was one motel of note. Adelaide was a place of trilby hats and heavy suits for men, demure dresses, court shoes, stockings and perms for women. It was, though, a tight-knit community, accustomed to the self-help ethic, and it could be unexpectedly daring.

Adelaide comes alive at festival time – a performer from Slack Taxi Theatre | GRANT NOWELL

Adelaide was also the home of Professor John Bishop and Sir Lloyd Dumas. Bishop was the son of a saddler in the tiny coastal town of Aldinga. He studied music at the University of Adelaide and the Royal College of Music in London and was a successful conductor in New Zealand before taking charge of Adelaide's Elder Conservatorium in 1948. Dumas had been a copy boy and junior reporter on Adelaide's daily *Advertiser*. He became a senior Melbourne journalist, press secretary to the mercurial prime minister Billy Hughes, and, from 1929, chairman and managing director of the *Advertiser*.

Bishop started Australia's Music Camps and the Australian Youth Orchestra. Dumas started Carols by Candlelight in Adelaide and was influential in the state's theatre movement and in bringing opera to the city.

In the late 1950s the two men coincidentally conceived the idea that Adelaide should mount an international arts festival. Bishop had been to the Edinburgh Festival and was much impressed. Dumas, struck by the similarities between the Scottish capital and antipodean Adelaide, had a similar idea and got in touch with the organisers, but was put off by the likely heavy losses.

Bishop went to see Dumas and the meeting rekindled enthusiasm. They decided it might be possible, with an underwriting guarantee of £15,000, to stage an Adelaide event. The local great and good were recruited at meetings in the Lord Mayor's parlour and the Adelaide Club, and the artistic director of the Edinburgh Festival, Ian Hunter, was brought out – at tourist rates, noted Sir Lloyd – to advise.

The curtains went up on the first Adelaide Festival in 1960. Twenty-five years later the British *Spectator* dared to say that Adelaide's forthcoming program made Edinburgh's festival seem 'staid and boring'. The student had upstaged its master. Bishop and Dumas were by no means the only begetters of the festival back in 1960, but it would probably never have happened without them. What they began has profoundly influenced the whole arts scene in Australia.

Their motives were not entirely altruistic. Perth's success in securing the 1958 Empire Games after Melbourne had staged the 1956 Olympics had riled the capital in the middle. Supporters thought that a festival would raise the city's profile and reputation, arguments that have become political mantras down the decades.

The role arts and other festivals can play in defining some aspect of a city is known the world over. Travellers flock to Bayreuth for Wagner, Salzburg for Mozart and, come to that, to Rio for Carnival, New Orleans for Mardi Gras, Melbourne for Moomba, and Sydney for the Gay and Lesbian Mardi Gras, just as they flocked centuries ago to Europe's medieval mystery plays, to the Circus Maximus in Rome and the original Olympics in Greece.

Adelaide's biennial three weeks in March, though, have a special status, partly because they aim to include everyone. The size and compactness of the place allow the festival to take over the city. This was true from the first festival, a modest affair that still managed to feature the Janacek String Quartet, the Dave Brubeck Quartet, the actor Sir Donald Wolfit and a collection of Turner masterpieces from London's Tate Gallery. It became even more true when the city built its Festival Centre in 1973 for a quite modest $20 million. The days of 1954, when Shakespeare's *Henry V* played in a tent on the parklands, suddenly seemed long ago.

Yet tents continue to be integral to the Adelaide Festival mood. One of its most popular features is Writers' Week, staged in marquees next to a military parade ground, where an international galaxy of novelists, poets, biographers and playwrights read and discuss their work and audiences listen free of charge.

Successive festival artistic directors, a colourful corps, have decorated the streets and staged every kind of performance in them. Like Edinburgh, the formal festival is allied with an even bigger and more eclectic Fringe, which has, if anything, an even more ravenous appetite for street parties and shows.

Festival and Fringe performances now number in the thousands, and even people who don't normally attend cultural events relish the variety, vitality and real or manufactured controversies.

The extent to which the festival takes over Adelaide was shown by an analysis of the 1996 jamboree which, not including the Fringe, staged 422 performances in

Flamma Flamma on the Torrens – opening night, 1998 Festival

22 venues with 1200 artists entertaining an audience of 700,000. Not including the free shows, that attendance represents seven out of ten of the total population.

In its almost four decades the festival has produced some unforgettable images. The South Australian-born dancer, actor and director Sir Robert Helpmann dazzled audiences in 1970 by bringing in the Warsaw Philharmonic, the English Opera Group with Benjamin Britten and Peter Pears, the Royal Shakespeare Company, Rudolf Nureyev and the Bartok String Quartet. No one who saw Peter Brook's international theatre group's staging of the Hindu epic *The Mahabarata* in a quarry in the foothills is ever likely to forget it. Jim Sharman made the Festival Centre itself a performer and used as a theme silhouettes of Australian cartoon strip characters. Into the new millennium the Adelaide Festival has its first hometown artistic director since Helpmann, the singer Robyn Archer, who swiftly got into the swing of things by saying she saw

At the Squeezebox – late night party venue for the 1998 Festival | ADELAIDE FESTIVAL

her debut event as 'precious, devotional, iconoclastic, celebratory, edgy, feral and fun'. Archer is also the festival's first woman director.

The Adelaide Festival has spawned that sincerest form of flattery, imitation. Each Australian capital now stages a cultural equivalent and, as festivals elsewhere have grown in number and scope, this has produced a problem for the next century. Should Adelaide remain biennial or should it become an annual event?

Some of the organisers have argued that, even if audiences could be found, it would be too much to expect such quantity and quality on a yearly basis. This seemed to have become the conventional wisdom in South Australia's small, overlapping political and artistic worlds when, like one of those races in which an unexpected horse suddenly pulls out and takes on the leaders, what had been happening in the Barossa came to the fore. The Barossa Music Festival has been one of the success stories of the nineties.

The tents are packed at Adelaide Writers' Week

Again it was a tale of a few people. Musician John Russell believed that the Barossa's Lutheran churches, other halls and winery cellars made perfect venues for a music festival. He worked with Brenton Langbein, a leading South Australian violinist and conductor living in Switzerland, and David Wynn, a seminal figure in both wine and the arts, to stage an event of 22 concerts in 1990. The festival blossomed and is now annual, many times larger and embraces orchestral, chamber and choral music, dance, cabaret and jazz. From the outset the Barossa Music Festival drew overseas artists attracted by the music and wine combination, and is now attracting audiences from around Australia and overseas. Although the size and facilities of the Barossa must impose a limit on growth, the music festival seems destined to complement and equal Adelaide in March in esteem, importance and pleasure.

Given the pivotal importance of the Adelaide Festival it was virtually inevitable that South Australia would give itself a Festival State tag, proclaimed on car number plates and intoned by politicians in ritual panegyrics. The cap fitted so well that when alternatives were sought in the 1990s, none of them seemed as apt.

There are scores of other festivals on the South Australian calendar, ranging from glorified fetes to events of real substance. For 24 years what was Come Out, now the Australian Festival for Young People, or Take Over, has given South Australian schoolchildren the best of local, national and international theatre, music and dance. The world music event Womadelaide, Australia's foremost celebration of world music, brings contemporary and traditional musicians from across the globe to Botanic Park every other year. Regional festivals abound, such as the Cornish Festival in the triangle of towns at the top of Yorke Peninsula, where every two years the locals and visitors surrender to the pleasures of furry dancing, putting the slag stone, Celtic Games and drinking swanky.

South Australia boasts a German-style shooting carnival, the Schuetzenfest, and many other festivals celebrating the state's cultural mix. Each new year at the fishing centre of Port Lincoln, Tunarama, Australia's only festival dedicated to a fish is held. At Mount Compass, a hamlet in dairy country, each February they even have a mini-festival based around cow races.

When South Australians get too full of themselves – midway through the Adelaide Arts Festival or the Barossa Festival, for example – you might try reminding them that the national cow-pat throwing championships are also held in South Australia.

South Australia's arts festivals tend to be reported in terms of visiting performers. That is inevitable but it is also a pity because a glance at any program demonstrates the remarkable richness and diversity of local companies. If you are interested in modern dance then any word-association test with Adelaide will instantly elicit two names, Meryl

Barossa Music Festival, Oompah band at Tanunda, James Morrison at Barossa Valley Gourmet Weekend, Youth performers

Adelaide Chamber Orchestra, Land, Sea and Territory – Alive, Fringe performers, Paul Kelly at Womadelaide

Tankard and Leigh Warren. The Meryl Tankard Australian Dance Theatre and Leigh Warren and Dancers are leading contemporary dance groups with a string of international successes to their credit working from an Adelaide base.

Continuity of the state's artistic tradition was highlighted by a show constructed around its best-known artistic export, Sir Robert Helpmann, himself a former festival artistic director. Helpmann was a dancer, actor and producer

Each performed at the 1998 Adelaide Festival of Arts.

So too did the State Opera of South Australia, the State Theatre Company, the Adelaide Symphony Orchestra, the Adelaide Chamber Orchestra and Doppo Teatro, the nation's first professional bilingual theatre company.

with a genius for outrage. One of the state's provincial arts complexes, at Mount Gambier, is named after him and has a crowded year-round program.

In the 1970s and 1980s the South Australian Film Corporation seeded the astounding renaissance in Australian

Meryl Tankard Australian Dance Theatre | GRANT NOWELL

cinema with such productions as *Sunday Too Far Away*, *Picnic At Hanging Rock*, *Storm Boy*, *Breaker Morant*, *Gallipoli* and the *Mad Max* series. Sydney and to a lesser extent Melbourne took up the baton, but there is activity afoot here

continued, renewed, or simply new vigour. The State Theatre Company dwells in relative splendour in its permanent home at the Playhouse, part of the Festival Centre, which is about to undergo transformation and

once more, fuelled by the Oscar-winning success of *Shine*, directed by Adelaide's Scott Hicks, and other projects. Adelaide's post-production facilities and talents are recognised as being among the best around.

As with film, so in many of the arts there are signs of

upgrading. But South Australia also supports other companies, and when federal funding decisions led to hardships and closures in 1998, the state government issued a national invitation, backed by funding incentives, to establish a new contemporary theatre company in Adelaide.

The Art Gallery of South Australia on North Terrace, home to Australia's largest colonial art collection, is revelling in high, wide and handsome extensions that have hugely increased its hanging space. The South Australian Museum is being upgraded to display its outstanding Indigenous artefacts collection. Tandanya Aboriginal Cultural Institute exhibits works of contemporary Aboriginal artists. But there are at least a dozen other galleries, some with a level of government support, most self-supporting, that exhibit the work of international and local artists throughout the year. Adelaide's Jam Factory has for decades now nurtured the careers of South Australian craftspeople, who have their own professional body, Craftsouth. I once tried an informal census of the number of nationally recognised visual artists and craftspeople at work in the state, got to more than 200 and gave up.

South Australian children's book authors, illustrators and publishers continue to delight international readerships, following in the footsteps of luminaries such as Colin Thiele and Max Fatchen. As book publishing becomes more and more a game played by multinational companies, a couple of local, independent publishing houses battle on, exporting rights and products. Adelaide has a Writers' Centre to encourage, inform and educate its scribblers, and is home to Australia's longest-running community poetry reading group, Friendly Street. The city's free arts and politics monthly, the *Adelaide Review*, has been much emulated interstate, and young people's street magazines flourish in a town that produced some of the nation's pop and rock icons, such as Paul Kelly and Jimmy Barnes. Local bands play in pubs and clubs across the state. Multimedia producers and visual artists and writers are making their ethereal presence felt. Literary and arts festivals are held in an increasing number of country centres.

The arts in South Australia are as much an abiding part of the place as the landscape itself. Some talents, such as Helpmann and actor Keith Michell, go away and largely stay away. Some, such as the 1998 and 2000 festival artistic director and performer Robyn Archer, leave but regularly return. Scott Hicks manages literally to have the best of both worlds while others stay because of what a writer in the *Observer* called 'the sense of exhilaration'.

Perhaps you have not heard of Jan Owen. A South Australian, she worked as a librarian and began writing poetry in the late 1970s. She has been widely published and won several awards. But poetry these days reaches only a small audience, so her evocations of growing up in Adelaide in a collection called *Blackberry Season* have not reached the readership they deserve. Jan Owen, though, as much as Scott Hicks and State Theatre, exemplifies the stream of artistic creativity which runs through the place.

Whenever this subject is raised someone always sprouts that old cliché 'State of the Arts'. For me it's more like a garden where you are always able to come across the unexpected.

'In the arts, it's about being prepared to invent and follow ideas fearlessly'

Off-shore praise is fine, but it's the domestic hyperbole – especially about our arts and cultural life – that Rob Brookman finds uncomfortable and, frankly, un-South Australian.

Lantern sculptures by North Adelaide School of Art light up *Flamma Flamma* at the 1998 Festival opening | BEN SEARCY

Brookman, who has been involved in the arts in South Australia for twenty-five years, including acting as artistic director of the 1993 Adelaide Festival, says this cheer-leading attitude probably stems from a belief that 'special things about the state' must be seized upon and paraded. 'You know – because we've got the best festival, we must, therefore, be the leading state for the arts in Australia.

'I think it's pointless, and I think it's a very un-South Australian attitude. If there is anything that characterises what's good about South Australia, especially in the arts, it's to do with being prepared to invent and follow new ideas fearlessly, without any particular regard to what is going on anywhere else.'

Brookman harks back to South Australia's settlement by non-conforming colonists to explain the state's contemporary disposition. 'There has always been a preparedness to go it alone. If you look at the origins of the Adelaide Festival, that is a real case of people saying, "That's a good idea. Let's do it," as opposed to people saying, "That's a good idea. Now let's think of all the reasons why we can't do it."

'The Festival remains one of the greatest festivals anywhere in the world. We don't have to say it's the best in Australia or the southern hemisphere, it's simply one of the best in the world.'

The logistics of staging Wagner's *Ring* Cycle had defeated the Australian Opera and Victorian State Opera

Fringe parade 1998, Adelaide Symphony Orchestra on stage at Festival opening night 1998 | BEN SEARCY, RICHARD HUMPHRYS

companies, but South Australia 'outrageously' suggested it could stage a full cycle here every four years from 1998.

'For some interesting reason, maybe because it's tough, maybe because it's hard work, the people who are working in the arts industry area are prepared to fly an idea even if it is against the odds. They will push it until they find a group of like-minded folk,' Brookman says.

'The Ring was a great piece of lateral thinking. Why build a brand new opera here? That entrepreneurial edge that South Australia sometimes has made people say, "We don't have to build it, let's look around the world and find a really successful existing production and let's recreate that, and ship in the creative team."' Adelaide's version of the Ring is borrowed from Paris's pacesetting Chatelet Theatre.

Brookman believes that the construction of the Adelaide Festival Centre in 1973 was a defining moment for the arts in South Australia. A city that enjoyed a vigorous amateur tradition became one with an 'admirable' collection of symphony and chamber orchestras, and professional theatre, dance and opera companies.

It surprises many to learn that the Adelaide Festival Centre is the organisation most active in producing and presenting the arts in Australia. 'Right from the jump the Festival Centre had to take an entrepreneurial approach or accept that its venues would be dormant for more than half a year,' says Brookman, who in various roles managed the

At the 1997 Food and Wine Writers' Festival – 'Cucina Italiana' panel Rosa Matto, Mietta O'Donnell, Don Dunstan, Barbara Santich

centre's activities and artistic program for more than a decade.

Again out of necessity, the Festival Centre set up its own scenery workshop in Adelaide's northern suburbs. The workshop's designs and constructions are acknowledged as the best in Australia and the Asia-Pacific region. A recent coup was the task of designing and creating settings for the Madame Tussaud's Waxworks Museum – the biggest to leave the United Kingdom – that visited Melbourne, before travelling to Asia.

The centre's Dry Creek workshop credits have included *Sunset Boulevard, Miss Saigon, Cats, Hello Dolly, Phantom of the Opera, Les Miserables, Crazy for You* and *The King and I* – which won a Tony and toured to Broadway, while a second show will tour the United States – plus countless television, film, advertising and display productions.

For Brookman, South Australia's cultural life is tied to its climate, lifestyle, geography, Adelaide's heritage streetscapes and the 'willingness of the community to support it'.

'I'm quite proud Womadelaide is not a replica of other festivals elsewhere,' says Brookman, who brought the world music event to Adelaide. 'It's got its own atmosphere, it's got a distinctively Australian flavour. It's also got a particularly beautiful Adelaide environment – Botanic Park – in which to present it.'

The state's landscapes have become important settings for other cultural events. Barossa Valley residents believe the Barossa Music Festival is the ideal way to see their valley at its best in spring. The Adelaide Festival and Fringe rely on the backdrops of the city's parks and gardens for venues and its courtyards and outdoor gathering places for nightly carousing.

'What you remember about Edinburgh is battling your way through windswept streets to rush from one performance to another,' Brookman says. 'Whereas with the Adelaide Festival, the memories are of sitting and enjoying a fantastic supper looking out over the Torrens after you've been to a great show, enjoying balmy nights.

'People in Adelaide take it for granted because we live here. People from elsewhere go away raving. Well-behaved artists are expected to say 250 times a year, "This is definitely the nicest city I've been in," but it is, for example, accepted within the writing world that an invitation to

Work by artist Annette Bezor on show at Adelaide's Greenaway Art Gallery | CATHERINE GASMIER

Adelaide Writers' Week is a good gig and one that you should accept.

'It's not just the shows at the Festival, but the whole atmosphere. The city is completely overrun by the Festival and Fringe. I think that is one of the great distinctive strengths of Adelaide.'

Between festivals, Adelaide's arts diet is also healthy. 'I think in most other provincial cities the size of Adelaide, you would be struggling to find the cultural menu that this place provides,' Brookman says. 'If you wanted to, for instance, you could be out at the theatre every week of the year pretty much, and you'd see a cross-section of work that most other cities in Australia aren't seeing.'

Brookman says there is a 'real sense of community pride in the arts' in South Australia. 'For me, the Festival is the most special thing about this state – for a lot of other people, it might be wine – but if you look around at what's special, it is the geography and landscape we live in, the abundance of wonderful produce, our way of educating ourselves through entertainment and enjoyment.

'Again, a lot of this goes back to attitudes engendered by the Festival. One of those is a belief that the audience is not dumb. You can provide entertainment that is challenging and adventurous all year round. Inevitably, you are not going to present the volume you'll see in New York, London or Paris; there isn't the population here. But as a microcosm, the state has a remarkable diversity.

'As long as we can hold on to the core infrastructure, there are events and arts organisations providing the drip of inspiration that allows another generation to come through and get into the area.

'This place has a very good way of disseminating arts to young people. As long as we can maintain those points of inspiration, there will be crops of people coming through who believe, "Look this is just what we do here." We have fantastic festivals, we have great theatre, we have terrific opera on our main stages, we enjoy a tremendous diversity of experiences and we watch a considerable number of them developed locally.

'As long as that is happening, we'll produce the individuals who'll produce the work.'

E-mail

And so, after nearly two years of frustrations and delays, it finally got down to where we would shoot our movie.

We were unanimous about one matter. We were not going to shoot it here in Devon where, someone took great glee in pointing out, it had rained for seventy one days out of the last ninety.

It looked like it had to be southern Europe somewhere, and even then we knew we couldn't count on it being summer when it was supposed to be.

The shooting script demanded orchards on Tuscan hills, towering cliffs, a remote town against a featureless horizon, a river (preferably with vineyards on its banks), brilliant blue water and fishing boats, a leafy street of grand old homes, an elegant city. And tons of blue sky, naturally.

'Anyone got any thoughts off the top?' Betina asked.

A few places came up and were discounted.

'Look people, we won't find everything for this script in one country, let alone one location,' a world-weary soul pointed out.

'I don't care where it is as long as it's warm and has a beach,' said someone else.

'Somalia?'

'Very cute.'

About a week later, after we'd talked endlessly about the merits of Spain, Sicily and Greece, we got an e-mail from Harry, a rough-cut Australian legendary for upsetting everyone from our chief executive down.

Everyone

Stop stuffing about. The place is South Australia. The bloke who made Shine *works out of there. Film-friendly place – they'll even welcome you sordid lot. Film Corporation in Adelaide – remember Ed Woodward in* Breaker Morant? *Strong arts culture – Adelaide Festival. Adelaide Hills orchards – you could be in Tuscany. Bloody huge river (Murray) with vineyards. Remote towns – plenty. High cliffs – Kangaroo Island. Blue water 'n boats – Port Lincoln. Grand old homes in leafy streets – at least five suburbs leap immediately into my frozen mind. Adelaide – elegant city. Blue sky – it'll make your face ache. Great crews – they've done features, lots of mini-series for OzTV. I tell you all this because the meetings are getting very boring and besides, Mum lives there and I can visit her on expenses. But don't let that influence you.*

Harry

PS Go on – admit it, I'm a bloody genius.

All right, we admit it. Harry's a genius. Mind you, we'll never admit it to his face. It's galling enough to think he'll be spending Christmas with his Mum.

On expenses.

Still from *Heaven's Burning* | DUO ART PRODUCTIONS

from Harry

'The film crews are returning to the streets'

The story of a piano-playing child prodigy who cracked up and spent a decade in an asylum has become a lightning rod for the South Australian film industry.

Although domestic and foreign industry interest had picked up before the box-office and Oscar success of *Shine*, Scott Hicks's movie has helped electrify the local scene. Overseas film distributors and production houses came sniffing around, hoping to find another *Shine*.

Ultrafilms shooting *Spank* in the city | MICK BRADLEY

The South Australian government recognised the injection *Shine* gave to the local economy – a $3.5 million jab – and returned the favour with $900,000 for new feature films and television productions. There is a 'sensation of "South Australia is back" in the national and international film community,' says Julia de Roeper, the

film in the Cannes Film Festival since 1980); Craig Lahiff (*Heaven's Burning*); Mario Andreacchio *(Napoleon* and *The Real McCaw)*; and several intrepid producers.

Other Australian film-makers such as Paul Cox, whose film *Lust and Revenge* was shot entirely in Adelaide, have long used the city to wrap up their post-production work.

South Australian Film Corporation's marketing manager. '*Shine* alone would not have created the positive attitude towards South Australia that there now is, particularly overseas,' says Judith McCann, the Corporation's chief executive, pointing to the recent success of other independent South Australian film-makers including Rolf de Heer (*Bad Boy Bubby* and *The Quiet Room* – the first local

McCann says that South Australia's film industry has a reputation for creative talent and risk-taking. 'What remains is a very passionate film industry with an enormous amount of integrity. It is not an industry that is jaded, and it hasn't become completely driven by the almighty dollar. People actually take pride in their craft and that's something the Film Corporation tries to nurture.'

Making ready to film in North Adelaide – actor Tori Dixon-Whittle MICK BRADLEY

about what is coming out of South Australia because we have significant directors who have their individual styles. The future of the South Australian industry lies in continuing to make films that tell our own stories.'

South Australia last had a real foothold in the national film industry in the 1970s – its halcyon period – when the entire state seemed like one big film set. Now, the film crews are returning to the city's streets. 'Word going around is that it has become very hard to do it in Sydney, with its congested metropolis. People are thinking, Gee, it would be really nice to make films back in SA,' McCann says.

And not just big feature films. Small features, documen-

production, along with commercials and music videos. Film-making across Australia is fashionable with young people and short films are popular, economical to make and are finding new audiences. But instant success stories – without the hard slog and patience – are few.

Scott Hicks worked for ten years before he started making *Shine*, and he always envisaged that he would film in Adelaide. In fact, he used his own street in the suburb of College Park as a location for a pivotal scene. Another exterior, a grand Victorian wedding-cake mansion, was spotted by Hicks on an early-morning bike-ride.

'Shooting in Adelaide was economical,' Hicks says.

'Crews can shift and set up several times a day, as locations are barely twenty minutes apart.

South Australia has twenty-five years' experience in film-making and a framework of value add-ons: catering firms with reputations for hearty crew meals, veteran stunt crews, animal handlers and wranglers, costume-makers and exceptional post-production and mixing facilities. Then there are the unspoilt urban and rural landscapes and the priceless attitude of Adelaide's citizens.

When back-to-back films were being made in the inner city, Adelaide City Council – traditionally considered a recalcitrant beast – decided it had better draft a 'firm policy' so that productions were not tied up in red tape. Even the Lord Mayor vacated his Town Hall office so Paul Cox could use it for *Lust and Revenge*.

Hicks describes it as Adelaide's 'generosity of spirit'. 'That's an enormous hidden asset. In Sydney and Melbourne, people are rather jaded and fed up with the whole idea.'

Hollywood may be casting its eye Adelaide's way and European and Japanese backers showing interest, but the South Australian Film Corporation remains central to the industry's development.

After an emphasis on television production in the 1980s, the Film Corporation – the oldest government-funded film agency in the country – shed its producing role

Conga! MICK BRADLEY

Crew and cast get a lift | VICKI BRADLEY

to become a financier for local films, telemovies, documentaries, short films and animation. The Corporation was determined that *Shine* would be made in South Australia and negotiated a state government loan – since paid back in full – to ensure it happened.

The Corporation's annual budget of $600,000 for production investment may be the cost of a Hollywood star's trailer but it's what the Film Corp chooses to do with its money that matters. 'We'll be doing the industry a great disservice if we don't continue to encourage and nurture the creative talent South Australia has got,' de Roeper says.

'It's called working miracles,' adds McCann. 'It's trying to pick winners out of the vast number of projects that are presented each year. Of the money that goes into making films in South Australia, less than ten per cent is local. The rest of it is coming from interstate and overseas. That in itself represents an enormous endorsement by market investors who are saying, "Yes, we want to take the risk."'

McCann, who hails from Canada and worked in New Zealand, says, 'South Australia's is an extraordinarily talented industry that deserves a greater amount of investment. Cinema is not dead, despite everyone's predictions. New opportunities are growing, and with the state-of-the-art sound facilities and companies we've got here there's no limit to what South Australia can do.'

Hey, who took my lighter? – actor Vince Poletto

8 sport in the south

Everyone agreed that 1997 was one of those years. Asian economies went into near meltdown. Tony Blair's new Labour government swept aside a generational grip on power by the Conservatives in Britain. World leaders fretted about global warming. In South Australia, though, many people regarded these as supporting acts to the main event. For this was the Year Of The Crows.

First premiership for the Adelaide Football Club, 1997 | DON McLENNAN

This was the year that the first Adelaide team in the Australian Football League won the grand final, beating a Melbourne team, St Kilda, at the Melbourne Cricket Ground, Australia's most sacred sporting site. Adelaide seemed like a ghost town for the duration of the telecast. Days later the crowd in King William Street at the official welcome for the players was the biggest, noisiest and happiest since the one that turned out to celebrate the end of the Second World War. Not a few people remarked that it was the sweetest revenge for the way the Victorian government had poached the Formula One Australian Grand Prix from Adelaide.

The Port Adelaide club's entry into the AFL in 1997 meant that South Australia was home to the league's two most-supported teams. For five years, Adelaide had been jeered as a one-team town. Port Adelaide's leap onto the national stage immediately divided the state – with only a temporary lull in the bickering as the Crows flew through

Crows fans at Football Park in West Lakes | DARREN CENTOFANTI

the finals. There are people who barrack for Port and there is everybody else. The club born among the docklands arouses passions like no other, mainly due to its unparalled success; 127 years in the state's league and 34 premierships.

lead item on front pages and news bulletins. South Australia in the late 1990s is happily caught up in this frenzy. It was not by chance that, as they were travelling to and from Adelaide airport on their path to the premiership,

Power fans at Football Park | DARREN CENTOFANTI

Around the world sport has become part of popular culture to an extent unprecedented in history. Reasons range from you-are-there, ultra-sophisticated telecasts and megamillion sponsorships to concerns for lifestyle and health. Sport rivals and at times eclipses politics as the

the Crows players drove past a new sporting complex taking shape on the western fringes of the parklands.

Looked at overall, you are again struck by a recurring South Australian theme: it is extraordinary what a city of around a million, a state of about one and a half million people get up to. Nearly a third of its people aged over fifteen play some sort of sport every year.

The state's netball and basketball teams attract fanatical followings and have produced many national stars. Almost every community has sporting facilities at its heart. Golf courses with rough, asphalt greens called 'scrapes', and sun-baked tennis courts, can be found in the driest towns. Each weekend, thousands of men and women pull on football shorts, netball skirts or other sporting gear and drive hundreds of miles just to play a game. And when South Australians are not playing sport, it seems, they are busy watching elite practitioners. The newly formed Adelaide Rams won instant support in 1997 as part of the television-inspired national spread of Rugby League. Local soccer teams have a dedicated following and the game is no longer regarded as an ethnic eccentricity. Weekend and midweek race meetings are held on three metropolitan courses and a score of provincial tracks. Harness and greyhound racing have their own headquarters. Training and breeding are lucrative industries in their own right. At the Memorial Drive tennis courts, one half of the world's top doubles combination, Adelaide's Mark Woodforde, has lifted many a trophy. Each summer Adelaide Oval is packed shoulder-to-shoulder for a Test cricket match and rural South Australians descend on the oval to make 'the cricket' one of the calendar's social events.

While football was centre-stage in 1997 international

International cricket at Adelaide Oval | DON BRICE

Adelaide International Horse Trials in the parklands | BRYAN CHARLTON

attention and envy continued to focus on the Adelaide suburb of Henley Beach, home of the national cricket academy. It was set up in Sir Donald Bradman's home town – no coincidence that – a decade ago and has one of the other famous names of the game, Rodney Marsh, as its head coach. It is dedicated to producing the best – sport is one area where elitism in achievement is no sin – and more than a dozen of its graduates have already earned the baggy green cap of the Australian Test side.

The northern suburb of Gepps Cross was known for generations mainly as the home of an abattoir. Today it has a more glamorous identity thanks to its Superdrome cycling complex, where the world's best coach, Charlie Walsh, does for people on two wheels what Rod Marsh is doing for cricketers. Alongside the Superdrome is The Pines hockey stadium, a complex of comparable quality.

Through the South Australian Sports Institute, Adelaide is also national headquarters for the beach volleyball development program. SASI itself is the first state-based sports academy and has become a model for others.

Nor should we forget private ventures. Neil Crafter was an architect who played golf until the tail started to wag the dog and the Australian amateur team member launched a successful business planning golf resorts in Asia.

Round leather balls, oval leather balls, hard balls, soft balls, cricket balls, golf balls: you can be sure that as you read some of them will be in play somewhere in South Australia.

Netball stars Jenny Borlase and Katherine Hardy. Basketballer Rachel Sporn attacks for Adelaide Lightning | STEPHEN SANDERS

'Whoever said sport was more than a religion must have visited South Australia'

Was Colonel William Light Adelaide's first petanque player? There are those who are certain he must have been – and that Light really created Adelaide's ring of parklands to play petanque, the ancient French game of boule.

Training at the Adelaide Superdrome | MILTON WORDLEY

Waiting to bat in the northern suburbs

Phillip White, city resident, wine writer and founding member of the Adelaide petanque club the Feral Aussie Boullistes, says that the statue of Light overlooking the city is proof of the colonel's petanque prowess. Light, says White, has been captured in the perfect petanque pose: an arm outstretched as if he has just hurled a silver ball. The sculptor simply has forgotten to place a glass of wine in Light's other hand. Several petanque clubs have taken advantage of Light's legacy and now play in the parklands.

The game is one of a number of sports and recreational pursuits that contribute to the city's sporting soul in and around the parklands – there are soccer, rugby and cricket pitches, hockey fields, football ovals, tennis and netball courts, croquet and lawn bowls greens, horse-riding trails, a 36-hole golf course, an indoor aquatic centre and rowing on the River Torrens.

'I was dumbfounded to learn that there are 43 sports played in the parklands,' says Kathy Edwards, chief executive officer of Sport SA, the peak body representing state sporting associations. Instead of the thirty-odd sports that there were in this state around forty years ago, there are now 105!'

Whoever first said that sport was more than a religion must have visited South Australia. 'When you think that Australia won nine gold medals at the 1996 Atlanta Olympics and five came from South Australia, plus a silver

Taking aim in the parklands

A young lifesaver from the Grange Nippers

reputation for staging 'very good sporting events' and that the millions poured into upgrading the city's soccer stadium and building new athletics and netball venues were aimed at cementing this distinction. 'There are Australian and New Zealand athletes who would rather run here than anywhere else. If you take Sydney and Adelaide, there's no comparison. People don't like to go to Sydney for national championships because it's a big city and there isn't the same volunteer base as here. And it's the type of people we have here in South Australia: there is a mix of event managers with experience, who tend to be able to work *with* the volunteers in a way that doesn't make them feel like they are working *for* them. That gives a professional push to our own

and 11 bronze, that's not a bad result,' says Marg Ralston of the SA Olympic Council. 'Only about ten years ago people often claimed that when South Australian athletes went interstate, they tended to be defeated before they left. That's changed. I don't know whether it's because of the influx of national team competitions that all of a sudden we are starting to believe in ourselves. Look at the South Australian football teams, soccer, women's basketball and netball. It's absolutely wonderful – they are winning interstate. Adelaide is a proven international sporting environment. We just don't sell it enough.'

Kathy Edwards says that South Australia has a

at the Grange golf course

teams because they think, Hey, this is at home and we can do as well, or better, than everyone else.'

Edwards and Ralston agree that having the Australian Institute of Sport's cycling base and national cricket academy located in Adelaide has helped sharpen the state's sporting edge and focused outside attention on the city. But they credit the foundation of the South Australian Institute of Sport in the early 1980s – 'the first and best institute' – with setting professional benchmarks. Its first full-time coach, Charlie Walsh, became the national cycling coach. 'The SA Institute has played a marked role in the preparation of top-class atheletes,' Ralston says. 'At the 1984 Olympic Games, with our three gold medal-lists and silver medallists, if we'd been ranked in the order of nations, the SA Institute of Sport would have come twelfth. It was their first year and here was all this money being ploughed into a few people. But it paid off.'

Sport and recreation is a dynamic industry that actually contributes more to the state's economy than the mining industry, according to the government's Office for Recreation and Sport. A groundbreaking 1997 report, *The Business of Sport and Recreation: Not Just a Game*, found sport was a $650.5 million business in South Australia.

'We have a big challenge to sell the notion to the community that we are an industry,' says Kathy Edwards. 'We're very lightly government-funded in South Australia compared to the other states.' Yet, she says, the industry makes important contributions. 'For instance, if we stopped everyone here in South Australia from going to sport for one week it would cost the state government ten million dollars. It's unbelievable. If we got ten per cent more people playing sport it would improve our health budget in this state.

'People don't understand that by 2020 we will far outstrip any other industry in Australia. Then all of a sudden, they'll say, "Where did *they* come from?"'

International sporting events including the Australian Golf Open, the Adelaide International Horse Trials, the World Masters Rowing and pre-Olympic training and match practices bring exposure and tourist dollars.

The Business of Sport and Recreation report showed that South Australians' expenditure on sport and recreation was

Netball at Port Augusta | MILTON WORDLEY

higher than the national average, as were volunteer numbers and participation in sport and recreation – yet South Australia has a higher than average proportion of ageing people.

Office for Recreation and Sport economic and industry manager Jim Daly says that South Australia's participation rate should be even higher, especially among women. Marg Ralston says recent figures showed women remain in physical activity longer through aerobic exercise than anything else. Kathy Edwards says that while netball has the most participants in team sports, the growth sport to watch for women is soccer. South Australian women embrace sport and recreation for health and fitness reasons first, pleasure second. Men are the exact opposite. But the traditional images of Australian sport and recreation – Australian rules football, cricket and surfing – are changing, especially in South Australia. 'As a professional body, Sports SA has to be careful about promoting football and netball as the most popular sports, when really they've become popular because of the ease of access,' Edwards says.

As leisure time becomes rarer and working-week patterns change, more people are turning to gyms and off-beat sporting interests that break with the typical Australian mould. Canoe-polo, beach volleyball, abseiling, mountain bike-riding, and the latest – aqua jogging – are gaining in popularity. 'A lot of sports – archery, fencing, petanque – are becoming what I call "designer sports", where people are being attracted to try them,' Edwards says.

She views the recent popularity of basketball and other sports as 'the mood of the moment and I can see that movement – it's been with us now for three or four years – already moving away.' Rugby League, however, will continue to grow because of its development as a school-based sport.

The challenge for South Australian sports is coping with life after the Sydney Olympics in 2000, say both Ralston and Edwards. 'I think we've got to be careful that we have events that will go on after Sydney 2000 for people to be involved in,' Ralston says. Edwards says it is imperative that South Australia develops a sporting plan, especially for non-Olympic sports, which looks past 2000.

quiet dynamism

'South Australia attracts more research funding, per capita, than any other state'

Mary O'Kane is recounting a conversation between the vice-chancellors of South Australia's three universities and a delegation of government and university officials from the German state of Baden-Württemberg. The visitors from the wealthy German region came to Adelaide to sign a government-to-government agreement with South Australia to collaborate on student academic exchanges.

Botanical research and study at the Waite Campus of the University of Adelaide | DARREN CENTOFANTI

O'Kane, the University of Adelaide's first female vice-chancellor – and one of the youngest ever appointed in Australia – said that the vice-chancellors discovered why South Australia was so appealing to the Germans: 'While they liked our higher education system, they saw us as an important pathway to Asia. I found that very illuminating.'

postgraduate courses, which are usually completed in Adelaide. Students come from Malaysia, Thailand, Hong Kong, Singapore, Vietnam, China, and also South Africa.

It is little known outside university circles, says O'Kane, that South Australia attracts more research funding per capita than any other state in Australia. She

But the news is hardly surprising considering the groundwork already laid by South Australia's three universities – Adelaide, Flinders and South Australia – in setting up off-shore campuses and joint ventures with Asian universities. The combined total export earnings of the three universities exceed $50 million, mostly from overseas students. Each university offers various degrees and some

refers to the universities as the 'powerhouses of the state's knowledge production'.

Anecdotal evidence has always suggested that the universities make an invaluable contribution to the state's economy. The first in-depth tally revealed that they earned more than $1 billion each year – including about 25 per cent of South Australia's research and development expenditure.

Graphic Design students from the City West Campus of the University of South Australia mount an exhibition

'Adelaide University is one of the top two research-intensive universities in the country. This has a lot to do with how we value knowledge in this state,' O'Kane says. 'It's this sense of: "We are living on the edge of the desert, we've got a few industries here and we've really got to make those industries work for us." We don't have the big capital cities, we don't have the tropical lifestyles. There's a feeling that you must be creative here.'

O'Kane says that South Australia has a long tradition of valuing education. 'Take a trip up North Terrace and you get the sense that Adelaide is a higher-education and arts-related town. There's this wonderful grouping on North Terrace of university, art gallery, museum and so on – it's stunning. The fact that it's all along one strip makes it really obvious in a short walk how dedicated the city is to learning.'

The University of Adelaide was founded by the colony's citizens in 1874. Flinders University was established in 1965, and the University of South Australia in 1991, from the merger of tertiary institutions with origins in the previous century.

The universities, of course, don't tell the whole story of tertiary education in South Australia. Adelaide has long been recognised as a major centre of hospitality training. The Regency Hotel School sets national benchmarks for food preparation. The International College of Hotel Management in Adelaide is one of few schools in the Asia-Pacific region to offer the Swiss Hotels Association Management Diploma. Overseas airlines from as far away as South Korea and South Africa send their staff to Adelaide to train at the Australian Aviation College.

Thousands of students enrolled in the new Asia Pacific Education Centre are also expected to boost numbers at the Adelaide TAFE (Technical and Further Education) Institute in the city's West End. Adelaide TAFE is already South Australia's largest post-secondary institution with 21,000 full-time and part-time students on a postage-stamp site. Thousands more are enrolled in courses at metropolitan, Adelaide and country TAFE campuses.

The Adelaide TAFE has recently undergone a $21 million upgrade, one of several developments cementing the West End's new reputation as a tertiary education, information technology and arts precinct. The University of South Australia has opened its $50 million stage one City West campus, while across Light Square from the Adelaide Institute, work has begun on the new Centre for Performing Arts.

Mary O'Kane says that Adelaide can lay claim to being a genuine university town, having two of its universities on the edge of the central business district. 'Smaller cities mean universities can be located in the inner city, without the worry of high rents. You can actually have creative work happening in the heart of the city. With two of the three universities located in the city, we embark on a lot of cooperative ventures together.'

All three universities engage in collaborative research with South Australian public and private sector enterprises. This is viewed as crucial to industry innovation and growth in the state. Links concentrate on high-growth industries: information technology, telecommunications, multimedia, electronics, environmental remediation, agriculture and health. Projects include fuel-burning technology, new weather radar, genetic engineering, mineral exploration and advanced sonar technology.

South Australia's universities are complementary, O'Kane believes. Adelaide is a 'sandstone university', a traditional establishment focusing on knowledge creation and education for mainstream professions. The University of

South Australia is about 'applying knowledge quickly and vocational education for new professions such as librarianship, journalism and information technology'. Flinders University fits in between, with aspects of both plus a focus on nursing and education.

'People often point out that when you get very intense movements in intellectual knowledge it goes hand-in-hand with the creative arts. I think that is one of the interesting aspects of South Australia. The community places such a high value on the arts; culturally that's rather different to the rest of Australia,' O'Kane says.

O'Kane's priority is to make the University of Adelaide one of the world's leading universities within 25 years - a vision that she says can encompass all three universities.

'I believe it's achievable,' she says. The world's best universities, after all, are often found in provincial cities. 'I think that this place can become a capital for education and research, if it sets its mind to it. And it has got a great base to start from. It's got one of the great national universities, and I think the city can push on and have a big international presence.

'The University of Adelaide is well-known for its agricultural and biological knowledge - the Waite Agricultural Research Institute leads the southern hemisphere in agricultural research. I would like to see it happen more generally.'

Periodically, questions are raised over whether a city the size of Adelaide can support three universities, but amalgamation is a sensitive topic inside the institutions. O'Kane thinks that South Australia should exploit the universities' export potential and make them appealing to other universities for forging further links.

'We should really have natural links with other universities interstate and overseas. We need to keep a clearly focused eye on the future, and not get diverted. South Australia can be a leading international player, both in producing education material for export and providing a centre of the knowledge industry.

'Think what you would have if Adelaide was so famous that people were travelling here naturally, not because it's an overseas students' market but because it's a good place to study and do research. We've got the building blocks to do it and the price is right - it's not an expensive city to live in.'

Su Song's

For a moment, as the train clattered in and the farm workers spilled out, she desperately wanted to cry. She bit her lip instead. Burdened by the weight of her suitcase and the bulk of the child struggling inside her, she dragged herself aboard.

The train crawled south, carrying Su Song further away from her comforting past and closer to her uncertain future. When she returned she would be a mother, but what lay between then and now was an experience she could barely imagine.

By the time the train arrived in Kuala Lumpur it was dark. The heat and the din of the city traffic were stifling and as she waited for a taxi to take her to the hospital it began to roar with rain.

She arrived wet and near exhaustion, only to discover no one seemed to know she was coming. Eventually, after much confusion about who she was and why she was here (as if it wasn't obvious, she thought), she was told to wait.

She waited until midnight, when a nurse eventually came for her. The woman apologised for the wait, saying something about the staff shortage, then ushered Su Song and her suitcase into a huge lift which took them up to the maternity ward.

A little later, when she was in bed, a midwife came to see her. She had the most reassuring smile Su Song had ever seen. 'My name is Prajaub Thirana,' she said.

The midwife questioned Su Song gently about how she was feeling. She took her blood pressure, then felt her very carefully to establish the baby's position.

'You got here just in time.'

'Are you going to stay with me?' Su Song asked.

'When it's time and you go into the labour room, yes.'

'Are you sure you'll be with me?'

'Yes. And there'll be the doctor and the other nurses as well. Don't worry.'

The pregnant woman's eyes followed the midwife everywhere as she went confidently about her job. To Su Song, who had always worked at bent-over tasks in the village fields, it was a revelation. Eventually she summoned the courage to ask: 'Who taught you to do midwife work?'

'Some people from Adelaide.'

'I don't know that village. Is it near Alor Setar?'

'Goodness, no, it's a city in South Australia.'

'Did you go there to learn?'

'No, the teachers travelled from Adelaide to be with us here.'

Su Song went into labour at four o'clock that morning. Through her waves of pain and trenches of anxiety, her eyes remained fixed on Prajaub Thirana's face. She was convinced that if the midwife continued to smile she would survive.

She did, of course, and after more than five hours she gave birth to a beautiful baby girl. Her name is Prajaub Adelaide Song.

Mother and child | ANDY RASHEED

journey

'When IT companies learn to export, boy are they going to be dangerous!'

It has been called a 'nerd's sandpit'; a playground for computer heads and 'Netizens'. Ngapartji (pronounced Narpargee) is not just another trendy cybercafe in Adelaide's buzzing East End. It is the on-line gateway to South Australia's rapidly expanding multimedia sector. While restaurants spill patrons onto busy Rundle Street, behind the scenes are a cluster of small multimedia and information technology companies that, along with Ngapartji – an education, training and support centre – are enhancing the precinct's primary social activity.

At Ngapartji Cooperative Multimedia Centre MIKE ANNESE

'This is the environment where ideas are created, not in government offices and stodgy institutions,' says Ngapartji's managing director, Michael Harbison.

Government information technology chief Tim Waterhouse agrees. 'Building an industry support centre in the middle of a university or technology park is not going to work. When we talked to creative people, they said, "What I want is to be able to walk out and have a cup of coffee, meet my mates, have my meetings out on the footpath somewhere." So, it was a deliberate decision to put Ngapartji in a cafe society.' A second creative multimedia precinct is being developed at Hindmarsh west of the city.

Ngapartji is South Australia's Cooperative Multimedia Centre (CMC) – a collaboration of government, universities and private sector – and an early example of the state's commitment to becoming internationally recognised as a centre for excellence in multimedia development. This is one of six areas in the global information industry on which South Australia has chosen to concentrate.

'This is a large, complex, multi-faceted industry, most sectors of which are growing fast. Our view, based on international experience, is that places that succeed build clusters or critical masses of particular specialisations,' says Waterhouse.

'Our specialisations need to be based on our historical and potential strengths. We think Adelaide is better at creativity – which in turn leads to a conclusion that when we look at multimedia, we ought to focus on the creative end of that business. And Ngapartji is very much built around the idea of being creative.'

Harbison describes South Australia's multimedia companies as 'small, quick on their feet and very original. Size and proximity are not issues now. I'm haggling with a guy in Brazil and that costs me nothing. I can do it in my lunch hour.

'Software developments in South Australia are more oriented towards smaller projects rather than "bet the company" solutions. Our export activity is poised to explode. Everybody is still finding their way. When they learn to export, boy, are they going to be dangerous!'

Apart from multimedia, the other 'niches' identified in South Australia's IT2000 Vision are spatial information, online services, smart cards, information technology education, and operations support – attracting the 'back office' centres of national and multinational companies. The Westpac Bank, for example, handles all of its mortgages and loans in Australia from one centre in Adelaide that will eventually employ 900 people.

'At the big picture level, the most important challenges are to make sure that we understand this industry and where it's going, and that we have a visionary, aggressive plan for our place in it,' Waterhouse says. 'This is not an industry you can follow in. You have to lead.

'Otherwise, we'll become a market for other places

and be dominated by their products, services, and culture.'

This accent on global competition led to South Australia's government taking a radical step – some say gamble – by becoming the first anywhere to contract out the whole of government computer information services to the American giant Electronic Data Systems (EDS). The nine-year deal took 18 months to negotiate and sparked political wrangling, mainly over the secrecy of the contract and concern about small, local companies losing out to a big, foreign player. On the flipside, Waterhouse says that the nature of the IT industry means companies come and go and that while the EDS contract has forced a re-structuring of parts of the local IT industry, it has encouraged successful companies to grow faster and challenged those that were struggling.

'If we were to be seriously viewed as an IT location, it was important for us to have some multinational companies here doing more than sales and service,' Waterhouse says. 'It's nice to have IBM with an office on Greenhill Road with some sales people but they have that in every city. You actually have to say, "We do something different here. We are part of that corporation's production of intellectual property."

'There are hundreds of South Australian IT companies, many with interesting products, most of whom have problems getting them to markets. That is the beauty of having a company like EDS, which is not a manufacturer but a service company with a big sales channel.'

Under the terms of the contract, EDS is required to use the products or services of local IT companies; contribute funding to the Playford Centre, an IT industry support centre that provides business, product and marketing advice; and use its presence and employees in the Asia-Pacific region to help identify business opportunities for South Australians and market local IT products and services.

For Waterhouse, one of the most misunderstood aspects of this whole-of-government approach is the potential for operating 'seamless, integrated' services to the public, which does not want to deal with bureaucracy. 'One of the examples I give is this. Say you are on the board of a winemaking company that decides it wants to plant another hundred hectares of grapes in the Adelaide Hills. Today, you'd get a consultant in or someone in the company and they'd go around to all sorts of government departments and collect all sorts of information. And all that information exists in digital form, sometimes it's on people's PCs, sometimes it's on maps, or on sheets of paper scattered over desks.

'But the reality is you ought to be able to go to a screen and say, "Show me a map of the Adelaide Hills." Then you should be able to highlight those areas that have soil types suitable for growing vines; take off everything that is not on

potential sites. It will cost you five million dollars to buy them based on this information. These are the owners you have to negotiate with." You've changed a six-month process into a 30-minute one. It's incredibly empowering.'

Wine is an appropriate analogy, because it is that industry to which IT is increasingly compared, as the state's

a north-facing slope; take off everything that is zoned urban. Start sorting and sorting, because all that information is there: the zoning, the soil types, the rainfalls, where existing buildings are, you name it. You just keep going until you get three potential 100-hectare sites. Who owns them today? What did they pay for them? When? So, ten minutes later you can go back to the board and say, "Here are the three

next big success story. Defining the extent of the local IT industry is difficult, even for insiders. Where does it start, stop? What is the 'end product'? A recent survey of the information technology industries sector by the South Australian Centre for Economic Studies found that there were 696 companies in the state, with a combined worth of $890 million and a revenue growth of 28 per cent.

They employ about 7000 people with a further 4000 IT personnel employed in other sectors of the state's economy. Employment in IT is growing at a rate of 15 per cent per year and sustaining this growth requires a net addition of 850 graduates to the workforce from local universities.

One of the biggest challenges facing South Australia's three universities, thanks to a mixture of government, industry and university funding.

'IT companies will sometimes choose locations purely on the basis of available people. At the moment, the industry is probably insatiable,' Waterhouse says.

South Australia must overcome its own departure

IT industry is producing a lot more skilled people and educating the community in using new technology. With American IT companies lobbying their government to relax Green Card rules for skilled immigrants, places like South Australia are under increasing pressure to turn out a ready-made workforce. Five new professors in information technology fields are to be appointed across South Australia's culture. 'By their nature, most people in the IT industry want to be working at the leading edge,' he continues. 'So, making sure that we have globally relevant, leading work going on is really important. If our multimedia sector is thriving, then our multimedia developers are not going to leave. They're going to say, "No, I like it here because I bounce off everyone else down in the East End, or at Hindmarsh."'

9 on the cusp

In 1845 Francis Henry Faulding opened a pharmacy on Rundle Street in central Adelaide. The only part of the business he would recognise today is the name. F. H. Faulding & Co. Ltd has grown into a pharmaceutical and health-care company with an annual turnover of more than $1.5 billion with products marketed in over 50 countries. Its success is due in no small part to the attention and funding it gives to research and development.

Quality control testing at the Salisbury research laboratory of F.H. Faulding and Co. | FAULDING

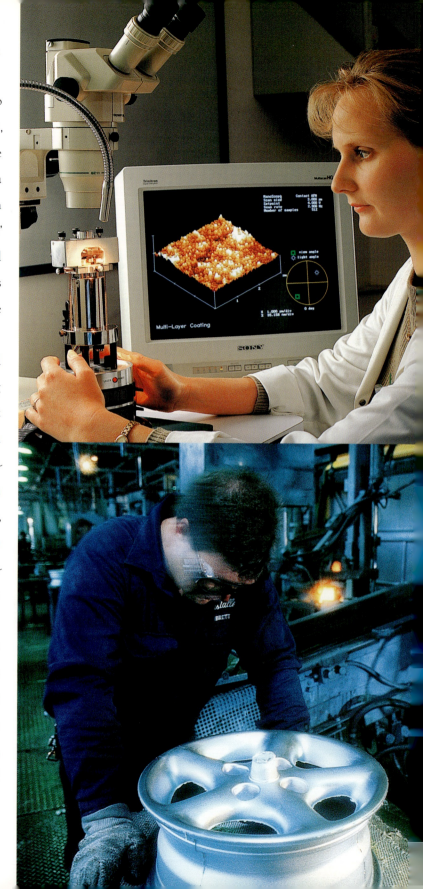

Research work at Sola Optical | SOLA OPTICAL

Smaller private South Australian businesses have also been creative in health-care fields. Back in 1970 Pat Crook, with her husband Don, had an idea. They would make sutures, generally known as stitches, for surgeons. As a result millions of people around the world have been sewn back together by South Australian products. The Crooks' Dynak company employs 50 people in an ultra-clean and sterile factory in suburban Adelaide, producing 2000 kinds of suture for all types of surgery and selling them to more than 20 countries worldwide.

Indeed in many areas South Australian medical research and development is now leading the world. Among the public institutes, the Renal Dialysis and Transplant Centre at the Queen Elizabeth Hospital at Woodville has an international reputation for its research into renal management. The Royal Adelaide Hospital conducts research in clinical sciences, biomechanics and biomedical engineering, while the Women's and Children's Hospital focuses on coronary risk factors, orthopaedic surgery, medical ultrasound and neurosurgery. Its most public face is the work done by its renowned Cranio Facial Unit.

Medical research contributes to South Australia's forward-looking manufacturing sector. In spite of adjustment problems in recent years, manufacturing is still the state's largest economic sector contributing more to the gross state product than mining, agriculture and construction combined. But, as in the case of Faulding and Dynak, the idea of

Manufacturing aluminium wheels for world markets | M. WORDLEY

Technological research for industry at Adelaide University M. WORLEY

manufacturing as straightforward metal bashing no longer equates so well with reality as the state manages an economy in transition and pursues sophisticated and profitable endeavours in industries such as electronics, information technology, defence and automotive components.

One in every seven South Australians relies on manufacturing for a job. Overall the manufacturing sector employs some 100,000 people responsible for an output of $5 billion. The automotive industry remains the state's biggest employer, and is an outstanding example of South Australia's effort to manufacture for the world. The shift from a domestic to an export economy is driving changes that focus on attaining skills and technology to meet international automotive quality standards. With a crucial 1997 federal government tariff decision resolved in the Australian industry's favour, local producers Mitsubishi and Holden are tooling up for a new period of growth. Industry executives and government are confident that exports will rise from $200 million in 1996 to $1.125 billion in 2000. Mitsubishi, which produces around 45,000 cars a year, employs 5300 people directly; Holden manufactures more than 100,000 cars and employs 4800 South Australians.

The newest player in the state's automotive industry is the components sector, the network of companies that make plastic mouldings, tyres, batteries, exhaust systems and seats. They export to markets in the USA, Japan, Europe, China,

Robotic assembly at Mitsubishi's Clovelly Park plant DEPT INDUSTRY & TRADE

India and South Korea and pump over $120 million a year into the South Australian economy.

One potent example of the importance of components to the state's economy-in-transition is Britax Rainsfords. A long-time supplier of interior and exterior rear-vision mirrors to the Australian automotive industry, Britax now earns half its income from exports. Global customers supplied with quality, stylish mirrors produced at the company's Adelaide facilities include Ford in the USA and Canada, and Mazda and Suzuki in Japan.

It comes as a surprise to most to learn that South Australia wins about a third of national spending on defence projects. On the river near Port Adelaide the Royal Australian Navy's new fleet of 3000-tonne Collins Class submarines, the most advanced conventionally powered submarine, is being built in a contract worth $5 billion. This has spawned the creation of satellite enterprises such as CelsiusTech, set up in 1990 to carry out the $400 million task of fitting the Navy's ANZAC frigates with the electronic equipment controlling their combat and radar systems.

The foundations of South Australia's defence industry were laid at the start of the Cold War – in the red sands of Woomera in the State's far north – with a joint British and Australian rocket-testing program that lasted more than 30 years. This investment led to the creation of what has since

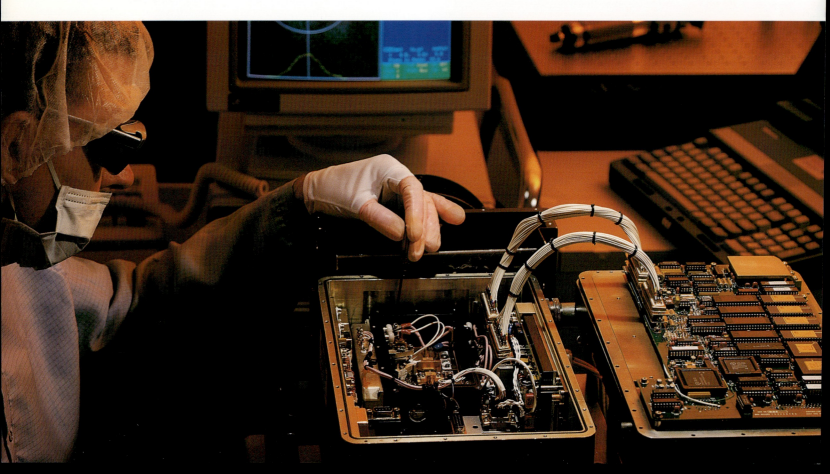

become known as the Defence Science and Technology Organisation (DSTO) at Salisbury, just north of Adelaide city, one of two national research sites.

The presence of the DSTO is credited with making South Australia the national leader in combat and weapon systems engineering, electronic warfare, information technology and surveillance systems. The Swedish Celsius group and British Aerospace Australia set up national headquarters near the DSTO. The Australian Submarine Corporation also came to Adelaide, and 35 small-to-medium companies specialising in the design and production of high-tech defence equipment and software have gradually joined in. The proximity of the DSTO has seen them cluster in the north of the city. The industry, not just in South Australia but Australia-wide, is driven by these small-to-medium companies. Defence is a South Australian industry worth $600 million and 20,000 jobs a year.

In the related electronics industry, one of the state's fastest-growing sectors, the Vision Systems company is one example of just how vigorously South Australians are pursuing and winning a slice of the global market.

Beginning in Adelaide in 1985 with a turnover of $1 million, Vision Systems has carved out a reputation as a developer and manufacturer of highly advanced surveillance and security systems. From its headquarters at Technology Park the company now turns over in excess of $100 million annually, with sales coming from all over the world. Vision Systems has also revolutionised hydrographic charting of coastal waters. Its Laser Airborne Depth Sounder system, which is already in service with the Royal Australian Navy, enables waters to be surveyed to a depth of 50 metres at the rate of 50 square kilometres every hour.

The electronics industry recently passed its $1 billion a year revenue mark with phenomenal growth rates of 20 per cent in income and 11 per cent in employment predicted to continue into the new century. When the government decided to compile a directory of defence and electronics companies and organisations it identified 480 of them.

South Australians have a proud tradition of solving problems, sometimes on a shoestring. Problem: How to open up communications across South Australia's vast outback. Enter Adelaide electrical engineer and wireless experimenter Alfred Traeger. In 1925 he invented the pedal wireless, a combined radio receiver and transmitter which he called a transceiver and operated with bicycle pedals to drive a small generator.

This legendary apparatus received and transmitted messages across distances of 1500 kilometres. The first user was the Royal Flying Doctor Service and later the equipment was used to transmit the School of the Air.

Problem: How to copy printed images from one paper surface on to another. Enter Ken Metcalf and Bob Wright of the Defence Standards Laboratories in Adelaide in 1952. They perfected the Xerographic technique using liquid developer, and their process not only enabled continuous tones to be reproduced but also led to the development of many new xerographic applications.

By 1967 the Defence Standards Laboratory had patented about 30 innovations in xerography using liquid developers and the process has been licensed for use in Australia and overseas. More recently, the world's first four-colour photocopier was developed at Technology Park.

Problem: How to provide more efficient and effective pain relief to cancer sufferers. Enter the scientists in the Salisbury laboratories of F.H. Faulding. They developed a revolutionary sustained-released technology which resulted in the drug Kapanol, first registered in August 1994. Taken orally, this product slowly releases morphine in the cancer patient to give sustained pain relief.

This little-known achievement is now changing the lives of cancer sufferers throughout the world. How appropriate that it was developed in the city that fostered the scientist Howard Florey, who carried out critical experiments that led to the discovery and mass production of penicillin.

Never mind what the economists, politicians and professional boosters say, I rather suspect that South Australians will cope with change and transition in the manufacturing base of their economy because among them are a surprising number of ingenious fidgets.

'The future of manufacturing is based on new ideas, new methods, new products'

When you are the best, you don't have to boast about it. If you produce something that is the best on the market, whether it be a Hills Hoist clothes line, Magna cars, pasta, a sunscreen or natural skin care products customers will beat a path to your door.

South Australia has a reputation for niche market goods with a world demand. Industry predictions say the value of South Australia's manufacturing exports will rise by 50 per cent – to nearly $7 billion – before 2005.

Sparks fly at Mitsubishi's Clovelly Park plant | MILTON WORDLEY

A check on the welding line MILTON WORDLEY

Ling says that South Australia's 'sleeper' industries – such as defence, commercial electronics and information technology – may have government and industry leaders in a lather but it is the automotive industry that remains crucial to the state. 'We are still very good at making cars in spite of what a lot of people think, because we've become leaner and meaner and more efficient,' he says. 'It's the basis, I think, of a lot of engineering skills. If you haven't got a good, basic industry like that, you don't have the apprentices and you don't have the developments in all those associated areas.'

Ling says that research and development in the automotive industry have outside applications that few people comprehend. Hills Industries, for example, makes

The fulfilment of that forecast cannot come too soon for the patriarch of the local manufacturing industry, Bob Ling. He has seen manufacturing's share of the state's workforce drop from 28 per cent to 14 per cent (about 100,000 people) 'in my lifetime'. Yet he remains adamant that this diverse sector holds the key to the state's future.

The active chairman and former managing director of Adelaide-based Hills Industries, Ling says the challenges to ensure the projected growth include 'bigger export markets, producing better goods cheaper, and overcoming the skills shortage'. With the continuing solid base of the automotive sector, he believes that the prospects are excellent.

Fitting the windstreen MILTON WORDLEY

Checking the steel rods

Rolling out steel at Hills Industries

Festival of Arts. A flaming hoist was pictured on the festival poster; giant hoists covered in bud lights decorated city parks; others became public sculptures and torches at night.

Hills Industries has now diversified into the electronics industry. Practical items like wheelbarrows, ladders and ironing tables have been married with high-tech electronic equipment, including electronic security systems and pay-TV satellite dishes. Hills employs around 1800 people and has worldwide sales of $300 million.

'The future of manufacturing is based on new ideas, new methods, new products and of course new equipment,' Ling says. 'We diversified in order to spread the risk, but we are concentrating on each of those manufacturing segments spectacle frames that are coated with a direct clone from lacquer finishes developed for the car industry. A former toolmaker is using knowledge from the automotive workshop to make special equipment that lengthens and shortens people's legs. 'People don't really realise that all these spin-offs help so many other industries. There are hundreds of other companies involving thousands of other people as a result of this one foundation industry,' Ling says.

Most Australians know Hills best for its Hills Hoist rotary clothes line, which has passed from invention to national icon. The cultural status of the Hills Hoist was cemented when it became the symbol of the 1996 Adelaide

and making sure that they are vertically integrated. Take the old-fashioned clothes line. We start with an eight-tonne coil and end up with a clothes line in a box. We do it all ourselves. That's the only way we can compete with imports.

'Unless you've got a product that is protected by patents or is unique, you have to be vertically integrated to be world-competitive.'

As tube and pipe makers and roll formers, Hills realised it could manufacture television antennas. 'From there we discovered that someone was needed to install the antennas and repair faulty television sets. That led us into electronics, and from there we expanded into communications and pay-TV. Hills will expand the electronics side – we think we can be competitive in that area where you have high-value items in a relatively small cubic volume.'

When asked about future manufacturing possibilities, Ling focuses on the virtues of manufacturing using South Australia's own raw materials. He is enthusiastic about the potential for producing plastic powders from resources found in the Cooper Basin. 'The government needs to bite the bullet. If we had a manufacturing facility producing raw plastic materials here, we would spawn a lot of other plastics industries. You might create 20,000 jobs over ten years.'

Ling also believes that it is time for South Australia to consider atomic energy to reduce the cost of power. 'We've got all the raw materials necessary. I don't see, personally, what's wrong with setting up one of these safe, atomic energy power stations somewhere up north of Port Augusta and also perhaps purifying sea water. Why don't we do that? I know that nuclear reactors can be an emotional subject but there is technology available these days to do it properly. And we need more water, especially for the wine industry to expand. It won't be terribly popular. But we've got the need, the resources and the knowledge.

Discussing government incentives to attract new businesses, Ling says: 'You have to do it. You won't get worthwhile investment otherwise. Once you've got the people here, you're about 60 per cent of the way to success. People won't leave unless organisations fail or something serious happens,' he says. The Hills headquarters in southern Adelaide were found for the company by former Premier, Sir Thomas Playford, the man credited with founding South Australia's post-war manufacturing industry on incentives.

'South Australia's big problem really is that we don't make enough products in sufficient numbers to compete on the world scene. As a result the economies of scale don't permit the use of the sort of equipment that some of the larger players in the world already have,' Ling says.

'That is why it is critical that the federal government gives proper encouragement, in the form of incentives, for industry to become world-competitive. I think the present state government is doing a fine job in creating a climate for good working conditions, with relatively competitive wages. They do assist with planning and the provision of buildings and so on, and they can give limited relief from payroll tax, so that altogether our total costs are competitive with those applying in many overseas countries. At one time Asian countries had low wages, but no equipment. They now have low wages and the best equipment. So it's harder to compete, but challenges are there to meet and beat.'

To achieve manufacturing targets, Ling says, there must be 'more creativity and innovation in every regard'. And more spent on research and development. 'Getting bigger markets means you can afford to buy the equipment that's necessary to produce each item cheaper. It's the old story: the more you make, the cheaper you make them.'

Fishing is banned at the head of Gulf St Vincent – the body of water that provides Adelaide with its spectacular line of beaches. An area of the Gulf is used by the Australian Army as a proving range for military ordnance, including artillery shells. When the testing is on, sometimes all week long, the booming can be heard for kilometres down either side of the Gulf. This is one face of Australia's defence industry presence in South Australia.

Another is the submariners who have been 'adopted' by the Duke of Brunswick, an old pub in the city. The submariners live near The Duke, which has renamed its front bar 'Collins' in honour of the submarines being built at the Outer Harbour base of the Australian Submarine Corporation.

Yet another face is the cluster of modern buildings that has sprung up on the northern outskirts of Adelaide. These discreet, designer buildings reveal little of their purpose, but they are the 'smart end' of the Australian Defence Industry.

Charles Rudder came to Adelaide because he could see limitless opportunities. An American with 35 years' experience in defence technology consulting and management, mainly in Asia and the Middle East, Rudder wants to unite the state's small-to-medium defence companies to compete for international contracts.

'We are trying to ensure that the South Australian defence industry serves the Australian Defence Forces appropriately, is profitable, and has a greater presence in the market place. If we can accomplish those, it will be a very healthy, thriving industry,' he says.

In only two years, Rudder has observed that 'the industry is very important to South Australia but there is going to be a lot of work to make it what it can be.'

'The companies here are too small and they can't keep

A trainee at the Clipsal factory of Gerard Industries | CLIPSAL

up with the giants coming in,' he says. The global defence industry is in decline after the end of the Cold War, heightening international competition for the remaining contracts. Compared to other countries, Australia has a flat defence budget and a federal government that believes defence procurement will be conducted on a level playing field, leading to intense interest from foreign companies.

'You can't see any one company in South Australia larger company. In that way we can focus on seeking, if not the whole product, at least a very strong influence on the product. Teaming of defence companies is being advocated all over the world as the way ahead. My opinion is that the industry is not going to make it unless that happens.'

The South Australian and Australian defence industries and the South Australian government have created a non-profit organisation aimed at ensuring local companies

outside of British Aerospace or the Australian Submarine Corporation, to a lesser extent Vision Systems and CelsiusTech, being able to take on prime contracts,' Rudder says. 'So foreign companies dominate the major contracts. Australian companies are put in the position of marketing to foreign ones.

'The need has come for collaboration between small companies so that they each look like a department of a remain world-competitive by collaborating on domestic and overseas projects. The Defence Teaming Centre, headed by Rudder, is situated alongside many of its members in Adelaide's Technology Park. 'The Defence Teaming Centre helps companies with marketing, helps them with bids but does not enter into their contracts,' Rudder says.

With work in the defence industry notoriously slow – the typical time lag between the conception and deployment

At the Australian Submarine Corporation's facility at Outer Harbour | AUSTRALIAN SUBMARINE CORPORATION, BRYAN CHARLTON

of a system can be up to 17 years – identifying and winning contracts in less than a year is understandably impossible. 'Can you imagine 30 to 40 companies in a meeting, many of them competitors? But they come to network and listen to what's going on in the organisation they have joined ... Previously they wouldn't do that. It's a cultural change.'

The Defence Teaming Centre can boast the signing in its first year of a cooperative working agreement with

of the companies want to do business here, and also, by way of Australia, in Asia. That seems to be the drawing card we have and we have to take advantage of it.'

Rudder says that another challenge for local companies is to export their innovative products to other countries. Defence companies also need to reinvest in research and development instead of relying solely on the federal government through the Defence Science and Technology Organisation.

defence companies based in Silicon Valley, California. 'We've signed a memorandum of understanding with an American lookalike, a space consortium – in fact we were patented after them. The purpose of the agreement is to foster collaboration with the American companies to do partnerships, teaming agreements, joint marketing, technology transfers, and help Australian companies enter the market place over there or have them come over here. A lot

'Most companies these days are stressing dual use. Products and technology can be designed for the military, and then with adaption applied to the commercial world, the civilian world.

'I predict the defence industry here will to become healthier over the next few years. I think you will find more jobs created. I choose to be here because I see the opportunities, I see the struggle to make it happen, I see companies and people willing to make it work.'

10 wide horizons

Perhaps the most compelling image of our age is that of planet earth taken from space, the blue-green ball wreathed in white clouds, beautiful, fragile and tiny.

We are a global village, a wired world. Yet South Australia, one of the few remaining places where you can be alone from horizon to horizon, still offers new frontiers. That is usually, and rightly, said as the prelude to a discussion about the challenging beauty and economic potential of the vast outback. But it is a paradox within a paradox that one of the hopes for the future of the driest state on the driest inhabited continent is fish farming. In a sense this is history repeated: South Australian oysters were a cultivated nineteenth-century delicacy. In the last years of the twentieth century, though, fish farming has become aquaculture. As well as the oysters, plumply succulent tuna, barramundi, trout and other fish are reared with the same tender care accorded to prize merino sheep. Customers in the sushi bars of Tokyo and Osaka have become very fond of the products of the tuna enclosures in Boston Bay off Port Lincoln.

Cattle droving at William Creek east of Coober Pedy | SA TOURISM

Meanwhile, South Australia's traditional fishing industry continues to expand: the export value of the state's famous – and succulent – southern rock lobster is growing at $10 million per year.

Leigh Creek and iron ore from the Middle Back Ranges behind Whyalla were vital to post-war industrialisation. The discovery that compares with them and with the early copper finds came in 1963 when the Santos company tapped into

Prawn trawling in Gulf St Vincent | PRIMARY INDUSTRIES AND RESOURCES SA/LENNIAN CONNELL

While most South Australians live on the fertile rim of their state, behind them is a desert that has yielded riches through the years. Huge copper deposits fuelled the first booms in the nineteenth century. Opal was discovered at Coober Pedy and Andamooka early this century. Coal from natural gas in what is now Australia's largest onshore petroleum province, the Cooper Basin. Natural gas, oil and related products are worth around $700 million a year and an exploration program planned to continue well into the new century could increase known reserves and the life of the field. Meanwhile, in the south-east, an area more usually associated with the state's vast timber industry, exploration has revealed reserves of oil and gas that await development.

No sooner had South Australians become accustomed to thinking of themselves as an oil producer than copper sprang back in the news when Western Mining Corporation announced the discovery of the huge Olympic Dam deposit at Roxby Downs. And not only copper; there were also gold, silver and uranium. Olympic Dam is already one of the world's biggest mines and WMC has embarked on a $1.5 billion further expansion. Commodity prices fluctuate, sometimes alarmingly, but it is forecast that the value of the copper alone could reach $700 million at the end of the century.

Then came news that South Australia might become a major gold producer as well. In the Gawler Craton, an area the size of several average nations that takes up much of the outback, and in the Olary region on the other side of the state, full-scale exploration is now in progress.

The country, though starkly beautiful, can be inhospitable and even dangerous. The valuable minerals are screened by sand and sediments. Now, however, they are penetrable by modern prospecting techniques, and a different kind of technology makes life quite enjoyable for the exploration crews.

In 1992 the largest regional geophysical search program ever undertaken in Australia began. The South Australian Exploration Initiative saw an armada of aircraft and vehicles criss-crossing the landscape, recording and probing. The three years after the commencement of the initiative saw the number of companies holding exploration licenses in South Australia double.

Gold is the main target, followed by copper and perhaps nickel. But the rocks under these tracts of sand could contain such exotic minerals as cobalt, chromium and platinum. Another prospect for the next century is a $1.2 billion outback iron and steel project based on colossal coal deposits beneath Lake Phillipson and iron ore in the Coober Pedy region. The Chamber of Mines and Energy believes the industry overall could double in the next decade. Since it already generates 50,000 jobs, pays wages of $1 billion and contributes almost 12 per cent of gross state product, talk of new frontiers is no mere figure of speech.

While the potential value of what might lie below the ground is staggering, further opportunities await downstream in the state's processing and refining facilities. This is important for the future of facilities like the Port Pirie smelter, for example, which produces more than 200,000 tonnes of lead and 400,000 of zinc each year, as well as quantities of silver, cathode copper and sulphuric acid.

Santos Ltd also has important downstream operations. It processes oil, LPG and condensate ready for shipping interstate and overseas at its Port Bonython plant, south of Whyalla on Eyre Peninsula. Whyalla, the state's second largest city, is home to the 'big Australian' BHP Steel's Long Products Division, one of the nation's industrial showcases, able to produce iron and steel products with outstanding efficiency.

In the metaphorical sense, even the state's farmers are finding new frontiers as they become more closely integrated in the food chain. This has been dubbed the agri-food approach. For instance the wheat in a packet of breakfast cereal in the supermarket is worth 10 to 15 times as much as the farmer gets. The potential to generate wealth all round is shown by the way locally grown products are being used by the San Remo Macaroni Company and Greenwheat Freekah. One of the nice oddities of the nineties has been the export of South Australian pasta to Italy.

Unexpected, too, was what happened to Grant Paech's pickles. He began producing pickled onions and jams from a cottage style outlet at Hahndorf in the Hans Heysen country of the Adelaide Hills. Word got around that these were

Logging at Mount Gambier Sawmill, Making pasta at San Remo Macaroni, Sheep at Bungaree Station, Combing mill at G.H. Michell & Sons factory

Bringing in tuna at Port Lincoln, Calendula flowers at Jurlique herb farm, Riverland apricots, Picking Adelaide Hills cherries

perfect pickles. Having been an early visitor to the shed where a small group of women were at work, I can testify that this was indeed a cottage industry. Demand grew and grew. Then Australia's airlines were shamed into ceasing to serve imported jams and to offer Beerenberg instead. Today Beerenberg relishes, jams and pickles are found in 16 countries and the firm supplies 400 luxury hotels in Australia and abroad.

At its farm at Mount Barker in the Hills, the Jurlique company grows herbs organically and biodynamically to use in its pure skin and body care products, now favoured by many women worldwide.

South Australian agriculture, of course, has since the nineteenth century been better-known for its sheep, cattle, wheat and barley than its pickles, berries and natural beauty products. Farmers from the state's vast arid northern region to its lush south-east supply growing interstate and international markets with premium lamb, beef, pork, goat and poultry, as well as 'new foods' such as kangaroo, emu and venison. The state's high-capacity abattoirs include the world's largest lamb-processing export facility.

South Australia's fibre industry, dominated by wool and tanned hides, aims to double its contribution to the state's economy to $1 billion per year by 2010. G.H. Michell and Sons, a South Australian company since 1870, is the nation's largest wool, cattle hide and sheep skin buyer, processor and exporter. Michell's success has been built on innovation since the days that founder Howard Michell decided to add value by cleaning wool in the local creek before exporting it, rather than simply shipping it off to England. Michell's products eventually feed the world's fashion industry, which in South Australia is represented by legends such as George Gross and Harry Who, the R.M.Williams company and Miss Gladys Sym Choon.

Somebody worked out that South Australia's dairy cattle yield the nation's highest annual milk production per cow – more than 5000 litres of it. Local quality cheese-making has joined olive oil production as one of the state's growth boutique industries.

The sunny Riverland is renowned for its citrus, pome and stone fruits, which can be found fresh or as juices in markets across Australia and overseas. The Riverland is also a main supplier to the state's marvellous dried fruit industry.

Orchards, market gardens and flower farms, along with associated processing plants, rim metropolitian Adelaide back into the hills and the far northern suburbs.

Perhaps the sweetest success story in South Australian food processing is that of Adelaide's Haigh's Chocolates. Established in 1915, Haigh's is now expanding its national-chain of retail outlets.

Whether it be underground, on the land or in the water, there aren't many places where the locals will greet the new millennium still exploring to find out what they have in their own back yard.

'South Australian farmers have a proud history of thinking outside the square'

For a state known as Australia's driest, it will probably be transport – not the whims of weather – that will ultimately determine the future of South Australia's rural sector.

Aldinga wheat farmer Roy Kelvin Deane TOBY RICHARDSON

Substantial growth in the rural economy past the turn of the century is being predicted by people like Gumeracha farmer Wayne Cornish, president of the South Australian Farmers' Federation. But his forecast hinges on the will to improve the state's transport infrastructure. 'Transport is critical. Everything in South Australia revolves around the

awaited extensions to the Adelaide Airport runway will mean more direct flights leaving fully loaded with goods stamped 'South Australia', but air freight is not economical for all products.

'The Adelaide-Darwin rail link would give us capability we haven't got,' Cornish says of the long-awaited

distances we have to deal with, the vagaries of the transport network and huge amount of taxation that applies to it,' Cornish says.

Adelaide has one of the most efficient sea ports in Australia but it is not the last port of call. Local foodstuffs loaded on ships have a shorter shelf-life than goods brought on board days later in ports to the east and west. Long-

project to link the mainland's northern and southern cities. 'We could beat most other Australian producers into Asia with fresh, quality-assured products that would have a minimum of travel time, despite the distances involved. The vast ship movements that are being envisaged out of Darwin mean we would only be a couple of days' sailing from destinations across the Asian and Pacific

Harvesting the crop | JON RICHARDSON

regions. This will help create an enormous marketing edge for South Australia.'

Another edge for rural production as far as Cornish is concerned is the State's 'clean, green, uncontaminated environment. We need to guard that jealously. We need to improve on that and we are,' he says.

'We haven't done the promotional job well enough. Country people need to see that urban communities are important, that it's a collective effort to butter the bread.

'There is a real need for South Australians to become 365-days-a-year suppliers. The only way to do this is to network and develop brands that are emblems of excellence,

Farmers are responsible for a third of South Australia's gross domestic product and more than 60 per cent of its export income. Few city folk understand the importance of the rural sector to the state's livelihood. When production from South Australia's farms, seas and forests is combined with the food industry (agri-food is the new term), some estimate that the earnings are as high as $8 billion.

and are absolutely pristine as far as quality is concerned.'

Cornish believes that South Australia is yet to grasp the full worth of 'value-adding', especially to its fresh food products, 'from a jobs point of view, freight point of view'. Most South Australian food products are shipped overseas in bulk. 'We simply are not doing enough with the product once it leaves the paddock,' Cornish says.

'Value-adding does not only mean you peel it, or cut it up, or freeze it, or put it in cans. Value-adding can be as easy as packaging fresh food in a more appropriate way. Packaging technology can add shelf-life and aid export to niche markets where fresh food is valued above canned or packaged varieties. It's about presentation and appealing to the end consumer. We don't understand that well enough yet and there's more development that needs to take place.'

Where the industry has developed – some say been revolutionised – is in adopting the attitude: 'From paddock to plate'. This agri-food approach has changed farming in South Australia forever. 'Farming now is a business; it's no longer a lifestyle. I think we've seen an extraordinary shift away from growers who saw themselves as merely producers of commodities. Now, they see themselves more and more as producers of products.

'The business management, research and development, and productivity increases have been amazing. The skills of South Australian farmers have increased tremendously. The range of South Australian cheeses being produced, for example, is just extraordinary. The dairy industry has done marvellously well in its industry development and product access. I think, in some ways, the dairy industry is a model of how marketing and product development needs to be tackled. Those who don't embrace the principles won't be in business in a few years.'

Cornish praises the enormous contribution to the state's rural sector of the Waite Agricultural Research Centre and the integrated and cooperative research centres – such as the Australian Wine Research Institute – based in a suburban precinct in the Adelaide foothills. Between 400 and 500 scientists and research staff are at the Waite precinct with another 250 around the state.

'If we step back and ask how the South Australian grain industry, for example, would have performed in the 1950s, 1960s or even 1970s under drought conditions, what the production potential in those days would have been compared to today, the answer is "light years apart". This is predominantly thanks to the dry-land farming research and development going on through our Centre of Excellence at the Waite. To be able to capture the benefit of little rain is very important to South Australia. We are world leaders in that sort of technology.

'National developments in the wine, dairy and livestock industries have been driven by South Australia. We have a proud history of thinking outside the square, and that has been to the benefit of the general economy of South Australia, not only the rural industry.'

While the rural sector is embracing change, its communities are declining at a frightening pace. 'We do have a problem in rural South Australia getting people back into the industry. We've been encouraging governments to increase incentives that allow young people to take up ownership of land, to encourage that generational transfer. But we haven't made it work well enough yet,' Cornish says.

Cornish, a fifth-generation South Australian farmer, is himself beset by outside pressures. His family's potato and livestock holding in the Adelaide Hills is being squeezed by development, land value rates and 'cultural shifts'. 'The pressures on the district are incredible and one wonders how long farming will last in those areas,' he says.

Nevertheless, Cornish believes an integrated agri-food industry will work to arrest the decline and provide employment in rural townships. The areas of growth he foresees are wine – 'fashionable at this stage and lucrative' – and the horticultural industry – 'tremendous growth, particularly irrigated horticulture'.

He says that an exciting development for the horticultural industry is the $50 million, 14-kilometre Bolivar to Virginia pipeline, which will carry treated sewage water to market gardeners and horticulturalists north of Adelaide. The value of food production in the Virginia triangle is tipped to double to $168 million, with 5800 new jobs created.

The grain industry, which has long played its part in supporting the South Australian economy, returned up to $1.3 billion in the past two years. Livestock has been 'in a bit of a downer' but wool 'is coming good again'.

'The reality is, I believe, that primary producers in South Australia, provided they meet the market needs, have a very bright future,' Cornish says. 'By early in the next century we'll see a significant lift in farm income. All studies indicate that.'

TOBY RICHARDSON

Mailman

The mailman landed and blew up a red dust cloud as he taxied in. As soon as he switched off the engines, the outback silence swamped him. He unlatched the cargo door, hauled out the canvas mail bag and the new motorcycle tyre for the homestead, then lugged them across to the 'mail box' – really an old Kelvinator refrigerator lying on its back.

As he dropped the mail-box door shut a voice called from the direction of another aircraft parked nearby. 'Whadaya reckon?'

'What do I reckon about what?'

'Is it gunna rain?'

The mailman looked up at the angry sky then called back to the invisible voice: 'Maybe.'

'Can you be a bit more vague?'

The mailman latched his cargo door and went across to the other aircraft. It was a single engine Cessna with a long needle-like probe sticking out of the tail. The voice, he discovered, belonged to a small, round, red-beard man who was reclining in the back of the Cessna amid a maze of seismic equipment, smoking a cigarette.

'Mind you don't blow us up.' The mailman tried to sound calm. The round man's cigarette was burning away beneath a big wing which also happened to be a fuel tank.

'She'll be right.'

'Doing a survey, are you?'

'Not right now. I'm having a smoke. But I'm gunna be.'

'I heard you blokes were out here somewhere.' The mailman was relieved to see the flying miner stub out his cigarette in the red dust on the floor of the Cessna.

'Mate, there's so much stuff under the ground out here a bloke can be lookin' for one thing and find something else. Like at that Olympic Dam. While they're busy getting the uranium out, the blokes keep tripping over so much gold and silver and copper it's frightenin'. Some of the largest known deposits.'

'Strewth. Reckon there's anything worth digging up around here?' the mailman asked.

'Well, it's a funny thing,' the flying miner said. 'The best data I've had in days was when I was taxiing along this strip about half an hour ago. All this gear started goin' off like a frog in a sock.'

'Fair dinkum?' The mailman sensed a leg pull.

'Too right. One day you might be tellin' your kids you once landed that mail plane of yours on top of the world's biggest gold mine.'

'That'd be a good yarn.'

'Funnier things have happened out here.'

'Well, I'd better get going.'

'Righto,' the flying miner said, lighting another cigarette right there under the big fuel tank.

As the mailman went back to his aircraft he hastened his step. Just in case.

Off the Birdsville Track | PAUL BLACKMORE

'Mining is not for the faint-hearted but there are great prizes out there'

The long interval between discoveries of major copper deposits in South Australia is seized on by mineral explorer Roy Woodall as he discusses the state's rich mineral heritage and future. 'The first thing you must realise is that South Australia, of all the states, is very much concealed by barren rocks and sand,' he says.

'How is it that after finding nothing for a hundred years, we were able to go out into the desert and find one of the world's greatest copper mines? Olympic Dam is not an ordinary copper mine – it is in the top ten in the world! You've got to wait until you've got the technology that allows you to prospect efficiently where you can't see the rock.'

chart of rock ages. 'These,' he says, tapping the next shade, 'have got a chance. There's some mineralisation in those and these,' even higher on the chart, 'are the most prospective. But unless those rocks are sticking out on the surface, there's nothing for the naked eye to see. It's all sand dunes. The early copper mines were found in these rocks here, near Kapunda

Leafing through layers of exploration maps, Woodall chooses one and fans his hand across much of South Australia's interior. 'All this is concealed. If you go down into the bush, you see nothing. That's a salt lake, nothing. Over here, nothing. This is what they call the Gawler Craton. But if you were down on the ground, nothing.

'All those rocks are barren,' he says, pointing to a colour

north-east of Adelaide and Moonta on Yorke Peninsula. But the rest of the country was almost impossible to explore for the early prospectors because they couldn't see it.'

Miners don't need eyes today. Machines can measure the magnetic properties of concealed rocks from thousands of metres above. Modern exploration technology is making the sand dunes penetrable.

In the late 1960s and early 1970s, Western Mining (now WMC) turned its attention to an area more than 500 kilometres north-north-west of Adelaide. Woodall, who ran WMC's mineral exploration division between 1967 and 1995, said clues in rocks already drilled in the area brought WMC to a pastoral lease called Roxby Downs.

were drilled before enough copper traces were found to keep the company interested.

The deep-cut holes, though, were still a kilometre away from the real ore body or 'treasure trove' as Woodall describes what became Olympic Dam. Its hidden wealth – not just copper but uranium, gold and silver products – was

Few South Australians today realise just how remarkable the discovery of Olympic Dam was. Woodall remembers 'how close we went to not even finding it'.

'The first hole got a bit of copper. The second – these holes were costing about $50,000 each – got nothing. The third got nothing, the fourth nothing. The fifth got a little bit. The sixth got nothing, the seventh nothing . . .' Ten holes

also about 350 metres below the sand dunes. 'So, if you'd gone there and drilled to 100 metres, you'd have found nothing,' Woodall says. 'If you'd gone there and drilled to 300 metres, you'd have found nothing. We drilled to 350 metres because we wanted to get through those barren rocks to the prospective rocks. And even then, we might have drilled there,' he says, his finger stabbing at a

Natural gas and ethane plant operated by Santos at Moomba in the Cooper Basin.

Night exploration drilling

map of Olympic Dam, 'rather than there, and missed it.'

Olympic Dam was discovered in 1975 and mining started in 1988. A $1.5 billion expansion of the mine has started. Output will increase from three million tonnes of ore per annum to 8.5 million tonnes. Woodall believes that there are about 3000 million tonnes of ore to be mined from Olympic Dam but also says that 'we certainly haven't found the limits of it'.

'This will be going on long after you and I, and our children, are dead. Most people have no comprehension of the enormous wealth that this deposit will generate. There's $600 million every year coming from just this. Somebody agrees to expand a shopping centre and spends $10 million and it's front-page news. We're spending $10 million a day,' he says, referring to the overall contribution of mining companies to the state's economy.

Woodall produces another map of Olympic Dam that superimposes its breadth across the city of Adelaide and its parklands. 'You can ask me "What's the future?" I say, "If something that big took a hundred years to find, how much more is there to be discovered hidden away?"

'I'm not saying that today we can go out there and find another Olympic Dam. We may need to improve our ability to measure the properties of concealed rocks. But that's where science is helping. It's irrational, when you look at the

At Tarcoola

people have come in and, using new technology, have started to find gold out there. This has fired imaginations. People realise that we have better tools to explore this sort of country. So they've decided to have a crack at it.

'It's not cheap exploration, it's not exploration for the faint-hearted, but there are great prizes out there. There are no other mines currently as lucrative as Olympic Dam but a lot of effort is being put into the Gawler Craton and the Curnamona Craton. I can't predict how long it will take somebody to find something; the minerals are concealed and the places have never been explored before. But the modern explorers have a real chance and the future's good.'

history of Olympic Dam, to say that we have found it all. Nearly the whole damn state is concealed.'

About $30 million a year is being spent on exploration in South Australia, especially in the Gawler Craton – a huge geological region stretching from the Eyre Peninsula, north above Coober Pedy to the shores of Gulf St Vincent – where there are prospects of gold, copper, nickel and zinc. The Curnamona Craton, in the state's east, is believed to be the 'next Broken Hill', one of the world's greatest lead deposits.

'It's all go at the moment,' Woodall says. 'The Mines and Energy department has provided this new magnetic map of the state showing where the concealed rocks are. Some

At the Boral Katnook gasfield in the south-east | MILTON WORDLEY

Megan Lloyd

Family legend has it my great-great-grandfather, a farmer from Cornwall named William Cleverdon, turned down an offer to return home to England to claim an inheritance.

Who could blame him? Cooped up in a musty basement flat, mid-winter in London, I once pined to float in the waters at Henley South on a day so hot the air would burn your nostrils; or to hear those perky Adelaide rosellas that love the city's leafy back yards and parklands. Or to drink the only beer so cold that it smokes, found in the members' bar of Adelaide Oval during the January Test cricket match.

This is the place I call home, where I have roots, networks of friends and family, a sense of belonging. Modern South Australia has been defined by thousands of people like me, descendants of waves of immigrants. All these people have a link to someone who made a conscious decision to come here. Adelaide is not the sort of place you simply pass through.

I hope that future generations will continue to experience the same sense of place. However, where once it seemed that only a minority or the advantaged left the state, mainly to travel, many families now experience the departure of their children for good.

South Australia is capable of proving itself resourceful and clever, as the many voices in this book testify. South Australians are sometimes falsely accused of being rigidly opposed to change. They are not frightened by modernity, just suspicious of it. The lifestyle that they fiercely protect carries the imprint of the woman I think of as the Mother of South Australia.

Catherine Helen Spence arrived in South Australia in 1839 as a 13-year-old. A teacher in her teenage years, she started writing for newspapers at just 16. She turned down two marriage proposals and continued writing – including the first novel published by an Australian woman.

Spence took on a public reform role that particularly targeted the care of children. She introduced a foster care system, helped establish kindergartens and the first government school for girls in Australia, and later battled for fair wages for female textile workers.

She became the first woman elected to a political position – as a representative to the 1897 convention that drafted a constitution for the new federation of Australian states. A few years earlier, as vice-president of the Women's Suffrage League, she had helped to win the vote for women in South Australia, the first place anywhere to give them the right to stand for office.

Catherine Helen Spence committed her life to change and breaking conventions. At celebrations to mark her 80th birthday in 1905, she gave a speech that continues to inspire me. She said, 'I am a new woman and I know it. I mean an awakened woman . . . awakened to a sense of capability and responsibility, not merely to the family and household but to the state; to be wise, not for her own selfish interests, but that the world may be glad she had been born.'

Tony Baker

Malcolm Kinnaird, executive chairman of the Kinhill Group, is one of Adelaide's great and good. He has built up an international business, sits on the business advisory council of the APEC Asia-Pacific economic grouping, is chairman of Adelaide Brighton Cement.

Kinnaird was musing about the state's future to an audience of his peers. The place was going through a necessary change. 'We are shifting, moving from a state with a few large enterprises to one with many small enterprises. We've got to look around for things that aren't big production numbers – small manufacturing exercises that aren't high volume but are very highly value-added,' he said.

South Australia is, undeniably, changing. Until quite recently that would have meant a skyline crowded with cranes. Although less tangible, the present change is more profound. In part it is a linking with the rest of the global village. When it does not matter for your work whether you are in the next room to your boss or client or on another continent, then the pure blue skies, the sea and sand, the accessible, 20-minute city, and the Mediterranean climate without the masses and pollution shift instantly to the credit side of the ledger.

Modern South Australia began in the mid-nineteenth century as an agrarian and resource extraction society. An industrial society was layered on top of that in the mid-twentieth century. Today, what has been anticipated for years is actually happening, and the transformation to a post-industrial community is underway. When it arrives, too many people will be insufficiently educated to cope with the change or at least to take full advantage of it. Such stresses are already apparent. But there will also be unrivalled opportunities – especially, as Malcolm Kinnaird says, for small-scale enterprises that capitalise on the state's natural advantages.

Most predictions wind up looking ludicrous. Instead let me wind up by repeating what has become my Adelaide-South Australian mantra.

Here is a community which faces no conceivable external threat; which is largely free of internal or communal tensions; which has a climate of varying degrees of Mediterranean; where the right of property is not merely respected but fiercely upheld by an independent judiciary; which is a parliamentary democracy that upholds the right of dissent; which can feed itself and export a vast surplus; which has abundant mineral resources and the confident expectation of more to come; which is defined by its neighbours in terms of a congenial lifestyle; which has some of the cleanest waters and clearest skies on the planet; where you can be alone from horizon to horizon or live in the small space of your own choice in a leafy suburb.

That is South Australia today. If this place does not have a grand future then I will eat my proverbial hat – and yours, too.

publisher's note

Wakefield Press wishes to thank the writers, editors, designers, photographers, typesetters and printers who worked on *South Australia: horizons beyond*. Your creativity, enthusiasm and hard work have made the book what it is. So many private and public organisations and individuals have given assistance and advice that we cannot thank them all by name here, but their contributions are warmly appreciated. Special thanks are due to consulting editors Jane Jose and Richard Watson for helping to shape the book, and to Andrew Male for helping with the photographers' briefs. The South Australian Department of Industry and Trade provided a research and development subsidy that made the project possible, and the Department of Premier and Cabinet placed a purchase order that allowed the publication to grow in scope. The South Australian Tourism Commission gave assistance in sourcing photographs. Wakefield Press thanks Wirra Wirra Vineyards and Arts South Australia for their continued support.

Wakefield Press
17 Rundle Street
Kent Town
South Australia 5067

First published 1998

Copyright © the publisher, designer, authors and photographers, 1998

All rights reserved. This book is copyright. Apart from any fair dealing for the purposes of private study, research, criticism or review, no part may be reproduced without written permission. Enquiries should be addressed to the publisher.

Directors: Michael Bollen and Stephanie Johnston
Editor: Michael Bollen
Editorial assistants: Gina Inverarity and Stephanie Santich
Design: Liz Nicholson, design BITE, Adelaide
Design assistance: Nick Stewart, design BITE, Adelaide
Typesetting: Clinton Ellicott, Mobros, Adelaide
Scanning, film and printing: Hyde Park Press, Adelaide

All photographs featured in this book have been credited to their copyright holders next to the captions except where space does not permit. Acknowledgements for these photographs are as follows:

Front cover: Colonel Light in red – South Australian Tourism Commission/Adam Bruzzone
Back cover: Crows premiership parade – Corporation of the City of Adelaide
Half-title page: Petanque in the parklands – Milton Wordley
Title page: Cycling in the Barossa – Milton Wordley
Page 40: Mick Bradley, both photographs
Page 41: (top to bottom) Mick Bradley, Milton Wordley
Page 54: (top to bottom, left to right) SA Tourism, SA Tourism, SA Tourism, Bryan Charlton
Page 55: SA Tourism, SA Tourism, Don McLennan, SA Tourism
Page 72: SA Tourism, both photographs
Page 73: Christo Reid, Nicholas Birks
Page 112: Milton Wordley, Richard Humphrys
Page 113: Richard Humphrys, both photographs
Page 134: SA Tourism, Richard Humphrys, SA Tourism, Andy Rasheed
Page 135: Tobin Lush, Adelaide Fringe, Grant Nowell, SA Tourism
Page 206: Milton Wordley, Milton Wordley, SA Tourism, G.H. Michell
Page 207: Milton Wordley, Jurlique International, Milton Wordley, Primary Industries and Resources SA/Lenman Connell
Postscripts page: Maureen Nampajinpa Hudson painting Crow Woman Dreaming – Catherine Gasmier

National Library of Australia cataloguing-in-publication entry
Baker, Tony (Anthony Edward)
South Australia: horizons beyond

ISBN 1 86254 422 0
ISBN 1 86254 425 5 (pbk.)

1. South Australia – Guidebooks.
I. Lloyd, Megan, 1966– . II. Title.

919.42304